Friendship

Life Together Resources

Building Character Together series

Authenticity: Living a Spiritually Healthy Life

Friendship: Living a Connected Life

Faith: Living a Transformed Life

Service: Living a Meaningful Life

Influence: Living a Contagious Life

Obedience: Living a Yielded Life

Doing Life Together series

Beginning Life Together

Connecting with God's Family

Growing to Be Like Christ

Developing Your SHAPE to Serve Others

Sharing Your Life Mission Every Day

Surrendering Your Life to God's Pleasure

Experiencing Christ Together series

Beginning in Christ Together

Connecting in Christ Together

Growing in Christ Together

Serving Like Christ Together

Sharing Christ Together

Surrendering to Christ Together

building
CHARACTER
together

FRIENDSHIP

living a
Connected
life

BRETT and DEE EASTMAN
TODD and DENISE WENDORFF

 ZONDERVAN®

ZONDERVAN.com/
AUTHOR**TRACKER**
follow your favorite authors

Friendship
Copyright © 2007 by Brett and Deanna Eastman, Todd and Denise Wendorff

Requests for information should be addressed to:

Zondervan, *Grand Rapids, Michigan 49530*

ISBN-10: 0-310-24991-0
ISBN-13: 978-0-310-24991-7

Interior design by Melissa Elenbaas

Printed in the United States of America

07 08 09 10 11 12 13 • 10 9 8 7 6 5 4 3 2 1

Contents

ACKNOWLEDGMENTS

It's been quite a ride ever since our first series was published back in 2002. Literally thousands of churches and small groups have studied the LIFE TOGETHER series to the tune of over two million copies sold. As we said back in our first series, "By the grace of God and a clear call on the hearts of a few, our dream has become a reality." Now, our dream has entered the realm of being beyond all that we could ask or imagine.

To see thousands and thousands of people step out to gather a few friends and do a Bible study with an easy-to-use DVD curriculum has been amazing. People have grown in their faith, introduced their friends to Christ, and found deeper connection with God. Thanks to God for planting this idea in our hearts. Thanks to all of those who took a risk by stepping out to lead a group for six weeks for the very first time. This has been truly amazing.

Once again, a great team was instrumental to creating this new series in community. From the start back at Saddleback with Todd and Denise Wendorff and Brett and Dee Eastman, the writing team has grown. Special thanks to John Fischer, yes, THE John Fischer, for writing all of the introductions to these studies. Also, thanks to our LIFE TOGETHER writing team: Pam Marotta, Peggy Matthews Rose, and Teri Haymaker. Last, but not least, thanks to Allen White for keeping this project on track and getting the ball in the net.

Thank you to our church families who have loved and supported us and helped us grow over the years. There are so many pastors, staff, and members that have taught us so much. We love you all.

Finally, thank you to our beloved families who have lived with us, laughed at us, and loved us through it all. We love doing our lives together with you.

OUTLINE OF EACH SESSION

Most people want to live a healthy, balanced spiritual life, but few achieve this by themselves. And most small groups struggle to balance all of God's purposes in their meetings. Groups tend to overemphasize one of the five purposes, perhaps fellowship or discipleship. Rarely is there a healthy balance that includes evangelism, ministry, and worship. That's why we've included all of these elements in this study so you can live a healthy, balanced spiritual life over time.

A typical group session will include the following:

CONNECTING WITH GOD'S FAMILY (FELLOWSHIP). The foundation for spiritual growth is an intimate connection with God and his family. A few people who really know you and who earn your trust provide a place to experience the life Jesus invites you to live. This section of each session typically offers you two options: You can get to know your whole group by using the icebreaker question, or you can check in with one or two group members — your spiritual partner(s) — for a deeper connection and encouragement in your spiritual journey.

GROWING TO BE LIKE CHRIST (DISCIPLESHIP). Here is where you come face-to-face with Scripture. In core passages you'll explore what the Bible teaches about character through the lives of God's people in Scripture. The focus won't be on accumulating information but on how we should live in light of the Word of God. We want to help you apply the Scriptures practically, creatively, and from your heart as well as your head. At the end of the day, allowing the timeless truths from God's Word to transform our lives in Christ is our greatest aim.

FOR DEEPER STUDY. If you want to dig deeper into more Bible passages about the topic at hand, we've provided additional passages and questions. Your group may choose to do study homework ahead of each meeting in order to cover more biblical material. Or you as an individual may choose to study the For Deeper Study passages on your own. If you prefer not to do study homework, the Growing section will

provide you with plenty to discuss within the group. These options allow individuals or the whole group to go deeper in their study, while still accommodating those who can't do homework.

You can record your discoveries in your journal. We encourage you to read some of your insights to a friend (spiritual partner) for accountability and support. Spiritual partners may check in each week over the phone, through email, or at the beginning of the group meeting.

DEVELOPING YOUR GIFTS TO SERVE OTHERS (MINISTRY). Jesus trained his disciples to discover and develop their gifts to serve others. God has designed you uniquely to serve him in a way no other person can. This section will help you discover and use your God-given design. It will also encourage your group to discover your unique design as a community. In this study, you'll put into practice what you've learned in the Bible study by taking a step to serve others. These simple steps will take your group on a faith journey that could change your lives forever.

SHARING YOUR LIFE MISSION EVERY DAY (EVANGELISM). Many people skip over this aspect of the Christian life because it's scary, relationally awkward, or simply too much work for their busy schedules. But Jesus wanted all of his disciples to help outsiders connect with him, to know him personally. This doesn't mean preaching on street corners. It could mean welcoming a few newcomers into your group, hosting a short-term group in your home, or walking through this study with a friend. In this study, you'll have an opportunity to go beyond Bible study to biblical living.

SURRENDERING YOUR LIFE FOR GOD'S PLEASURE (WORSHIP). God is most pleased by a heart that is fully his. Each group session will give you a chance to surrender your heart to God in prayer and worship. You may read a psalm together, share a page in your journal, or sing a song to close your meeting. (A Life Together Worship DVD/CD series, produced by Maranatha!, is available through www.lifetogether. com.) If you have never prayed aloud in a group before, no one will put pressure on you. Instead, you'll experience the support of others who are praying for you. This time will knit your hearts in community and help you surrender your hurts and dreams into the hands of the One who knows you best.

STUDY NOTES. This section provides background notes on the Bible passage(s) you examine in the Growing section. You may want to refer to these notes during your group meeting or as a reference for those doing additional study.

REFLECTIONS. Each week on the Reflections pages we provide Scriptures to read and reflect on between group meetings. We suggest you use this section to seek God at home throughout the week. This time at home should begin and end with prayer. Don't get in a hurry; take enough time to hear God's direction.

SUBGROUPS FOR DISCUSSION AND PRAYER. In some of the sessions of this series we have suggested you separate into groups of two to four for discussion or prayer. This is to assure greater participation and deeper discussion.

DAVID AND JONATHAN — FRIENDS FOR LIFE

I will always remember a time when, as a single young adult, one of my former roommates, who was in a college ministry five hundred miles away, got into some trouble. At the time, I was still working with a pastor who had mentored us both. When we found out about our brother in need, we both felt the situation warranted more than just a phone call. That's when we both got the same idea at the same time: *Let's get in the car and go see him without letting him know we're coming.* It meant ten hours each way and the trip down was going to have to be an all-nighter in order to work it into our schedules. No matter. Within an hour, we were on the road.

I'll never forget the look on our friend's face when we walked into his house the next morning and hugged him. I think we were there no more than three hours before we had to turn right around and head back. It was brief, but it was enough to help set him in the right direction, and though I don't think any of us remember what was said, we all remember that we were there. Our friendship and the Holy Spirit in us made us do it and that was the most important part. After all, isn't that what friends are for?

CONNECTING WITH GOD'S FAMILY   20 MIN.

Networking is a big word in today's world for the connections we make with others almost everywhere we go — in our workplace, school, church, carpools, gym, clubs, serving environments — wherever people share common passions. But while networking is a great way to establish contacts, true friendship goes deeper. No matter how they get started or what storms they might endure along the way, true friendship has permanence to it — one that often builds into relationships you simply cannot live without, like the one modeled for us in Scripture by David and Jonathan.

In this first session of six, we'll take our initial steps on a journey through genuine friendship, beginning with the story of David and Jonathan. We'll talk about what friendship is, where we find it, and how we can be authentic friends.

1. What are some of the qualities you consider important in a true friend? Write them here and share one or two with your group.

2. With any group, whether you are just forming or have been together for awhile, it's good to review and consider your shared values from time to time. You'll find a Small Group Agreement on pages 89–90 outlining those values we have found over the years to be the most useful in building and sustaining healthy, balanced groups. It's a good idea to pick one or two values you haven't focused on before to guide you through this series and help you build deeper friendships. If your group is new, you may also find helpful the Frequently Asked Questions section on pages 86–88.

    While you are working through the rest of this session, pass around a sheet of paper or one of you pass your study guide opened to the Small Group Roster on pages 117–118. Have everyone write down their contact information, then ask someone to make copies or type up a list with everyone's information and email it to the group this week.

3. We recommend that you rotate host homes on a regular basis and let the hosts lead the meeting. We've come to realize that healthy groups rotate leadership. This helps to develop every member's ability to shepherd a few people in a safe environment. Even Jesus gave others the opportunity to serve alongside him (Mark 6:30–44). Session two will explain how to set up a rotating schedule.

GROWING TO BE LIKE CHRIST   40 MIN.

Over the centuries, the powerful relationship shared by David and Jonathan has captured the hearts and imaginations of many authors, both secular and Christian. Its power is as mysterious as it is undeniable, representing the type of relationship all of us, at the core of our being, long to know. Where can we find this soul connection, someone who will love us unconditionally and without reservation?

Not long after David killed Goliath, Jonathan and David's relationship became an unsurpassed example of friendship in Scripture. As young men and at Jonathan's initiation, they sealed their commitment by entering into a covenant relationship (1 Samuel 18:1–4). Many of us may recall making pacts with our pals on childhood playgrounds, but this was something more. As the two would soon discover, friendship for them was about more than someone to hang out with or even a listening ear—for them, friendship literally became a matter of life or death.

When Prince Jonathan heard that his father, out of fear for his throne, was seeking David's life (1 Samuel 20:1–34), Jonathan faced an awful choice. Where should his loyalty lie—with his father and king, or with his friend? He loved them both.

For David, friendship with Jonathan would become a question of honoring their pledge (1 Samuel 20:35–42) years down the road. Long after Jonathan had died, after David had become king of Judah, David remembered his promise to take care of Jonathan's household. When he learned about the existence of Mephibosheth, Jonathan's crippled son, he made sure the young man was provided for his whole life through (2 Samuel 9:1–13).

Proverbs 18:24 tells us, "A man of many companions may come to ruin, but there is a friend who sticks closer than a brother." In the story of David and Jonathan, we witness a picture of this rare and genuine love. While most of us will not face the kinds of tests David and Jonathan confronted, their story offers great insight and challenge for us as we consider our own commitments within the community of Christ.

Read 1 Samuel 18:1–4:

> *After David had finished talking with Saul, Jonathan became one in spirit with David, and he loved him as himself. ²From that day Saul kept David with him and did not let him return to his father's house. ³And Jonathan made a covenant with David because he loved him as himself. ⁴Jonathan took off the robe he was wearing and gave it to David, along with his tunic, and even his sword, his bow and his belt.*

4. It's clear from 1 Samuel 18:1 that David and Jonathan were closer than ordinary friends. According to various Bible translations, Jonathan's soul was "knit" to that of David (NASB),

there was "an immediate bond of love between them, and they became the best of friends" (NLT), and "Jonathan became one in spirit with David, and he loved him as himself" (NIV). What do these various phrases tell you about the depth of their friendship? If any of you has another translation, read from it to expand your understanding of David and Jonathan's friendship.

5. In 1 Samuel 18:3, what did Jonathan decide to do? What prompted his decision?

   Has God ever prompted your heart to make a commitment to another believer in a similar way? One or two of you share your story briefly with the group.

6. In 1 Samuel 19:1–2, Jonathan disobeyed his father's command. Was he right to do so? What about his friendship with David do you think prompted this disobedience?

7. In today's world, what are some of the ways we establish and demonstrate a commitment to others?

8. In 1 Samuel 19:4, we see Jonathan defending David before the king. Imagine someone you loved and respected came against your close friend. How do you think you would respond?

9. Read 1 Samuel 20. In verse 4, Jonathan said to his friend, "Whatever you want me to do, I'll do for you." Has there ever been a situation in your life that required you to make such a sacrificial commitment for another? Share with the group. If this is a current situation on which you have not yet acted, ask the group to pray with you during the Surrendering prayer time that you would experience God's supernatural strength to give of yourself in a new capacity.

10. Many of us find that connecting with others on a deeper level is not easy. We may even have been hurt by reaching out, and so pulled back from seeking further fellowship. As you look through 1 Samuel chapters 18 and 20, count all the verses in which Jonathan pledges his love and commitment to David. Is there a person in your life toward whom you need to take a step of friendship this week? Ask God for an opportunity to connect with that person.

11. Read 1 Samuel 20:14 – 17, 42; 2 Samuel 9:1 – 13; 21:1 – 7. How did David demonstrate how seriously he took the covenant he entered into with Jonathan?

FOR DEEPER STUDY

You can learn more about David and Jonathan's relationship by reading 1 Samuel 13 – 14; 18:1 – 4; 19:1 – 6; and 20:1 – 42.

In 1 Samuel 20:1 – 3, David consults Jonathan regarding Saul's pursuit. How could this moment have potentially affected their friendship?

What did David understand that Jonathan could not yet see?

What test did David create in order to (1) guard his own safety, and (2) reveal to Jonathan Saul's treachery? See 1 Samuel 20:5–7.

How did Jonathan's answer in 1 Samuel 20:9 reveal the depth of his commitment to David?

Proverbs 17:17 says, "A friend loves at all times, and a brother is born for adversity." How do David and Jonathan exemplify this verse?

Describe a loyal friendship in your life.

DEVELOPING YOUR GIFTS TO SERVE OTHERS   10 MIN.

12. In 1 Samuel 23:16 we see that Jonathan encouraged and strengthened David in his faith in God. Is there someone you can encourage or strengthen "in the Lord"? Choose one way you can encourage him or her in God this week. Make a plan and follow up.

Who needs an encouraging word from you?

_____ (*Write name here*)

How can you help them "in God"? _____

Today, write a letter or make a phone call to someone demonstrating your commitment and encouraging him or her "in God." Be a Jonathan to a David in your life.

13. Developing your Christian life involves prayer, reading God's Word, and reflecting on what God is telling you through it. If you engage in these activities over the next six weeks, you will see growth. We have provided a Reflections section on pages 23–25 with selected Scripture for you to read and reflect upon. There is also a place for you to record your thoughts. This important habit will help you grow closer to God throughout this study.

14. Pair up with someone in your group. (We suggest that men partner with men and women with women.) This person will be your "spiritual partner" during this study. He or she doesn't have to be your best friend but will simply encourage you to complete any goals you set for yourself during the course of this study. Following through on a resolution is tough when you're on your own, but we've found it makes all the difference to have a partner cheering us on.

On pages 92–93 is a Personal Health Plan, a chart for keeping track of your spiritual progress. In the box that says "WHO are you connecting with spiritually?" write your partner's name. In the box that says "WHAT is your next step for growth?" write the step(s) you are choosing to work on during this study. You have now begun to address two of God's five purposes for your life! You can see that the health plan contains space for you to record the ups and downs of your progress each week in the column labeled "My Progress." And now with your spiritual partner you don't have to do it alone, but together with a friend.

Tell your partner what step(s) you chose. When you check in with your partner each week, the "Partner's Progress" column on this chart will provide a place to record your partner's progress in the goal he or she chose.

To help you use your Personal Health Plan, on pages 94–95 you'll find a completed health plan as an example. For now, don't worry about the WHERE, WHEN, and HOW questions on your health plan.

SHARING YOUR LIFE MISSION EVERY DAY   10 MIN.

God did not call us to live this life alone. Rather, we were created to be in relationship with others. God made us for friendships like that of David and Jonathan. It takes courage to love someone deeply. As the people around you face trials of many kinds, you, as a friend of God, have the unique privilege of spurring them on to become the men and women God has called them to be. In that way, you can make an eternal difference in their lives.

15. Perhaps God has brought you alongside someone who is seeking to know God in a personal way. Invite that person to visit your group. Pray for more opportunities to be with them in the way God is leading you. Trust him to guide you as you spend time with this person. Don't be discouraged if not every encounter appears to be successful. It is God's work. Write the name of the person you will begin to pray for below. During the Surrendering section, be sure to pray for them.

_____ (*Write name here*)

SURRENDERING YOUR LIFE FOR GOD'S PLEASURE   15–20 MIN.

16. Is there someone with whom you would like to be in a relationship like David and Jonathan's? Or is there someone you need to commit to, but fear has caused you to delay the commitment? Ask God to reveal his will for you in this area as you surrender your desires to him. If you need prayer about this, share with the group how you would like them to pray for you.

17. Allow everyone to answer this question: How can we pray for you this week? Be sure to write these requests on your Prayer and Praise Report on page 22.

STUDY NOTES

The soul of Jonathan as knit to the soul of David. This phrase in Hebrew is *nepesh niqsherah benepesh*, meaning "became one in spirit with." This is a sign of spiritual binding, a commitment of two persons, life on life, that forms a lifelong tie.

Jonathan loved him as himself. Some writers have commented that this reference points to a possible homosexual relationship between these two young men. But the use of the Hebrew *aheb* ("love") is not used to refer to that kind of relationship (see also 1 Samuel 20:17). It reveals a covenant relationship that unites David to the royal household. The word *yada*, meaning sexual union (see Genesis 19:5), is never used to describe David and Jonathan's love.

Stripped himself of his robe. This single act transferred Jonathan's heir-apparent status of the throne to David.

Was very fond of. (See 1 Samuel 19:1). The Hebrew word *chaphets* here means "to take pleasure in, to desire, to be pleased with." Saul expressed the same affection toward David in 1 Samuel 18:22. The context is not sexual, but a relational, emotional bonding.

Unfailing kindness like that of the LORD. (See 1 Samuel 20:14.) The Hebrew *hesed elohim*, or loving kindness of the Lord, denotes the greatest possible loyalty between two people. As God is loyal to us, Jonathan promised that same loyalty to David.

Between you and me forever. (See 1 Samuel 20:23.) This is the same kind of covenant relationship described between Jacob and Laban (Genesis 31:48–53). Covenant relationships lasted a lifetime.

PRAYER AND PRAISE REPORT

Briefly share your prayer requests with the large group, making notations below. Then gather in small groups of two to four to pray for each other.

Date: _____

PRAYER REQUESTS

_____

_____

_____

_____

_____

_____

_____

_____

_____

_____

_____

_____

PRAISE REPORT

_____

_____

_____

_____

_____

_____

_____

_____

REFLECTIONS

Each day read the daily verse(s) and give prayerful consideration to what you learn about God, his Spirit, and his place in your life. Then record your thoughts, insights, or prayer in the Reflect section. On day six record a summary of what you have learned over the entire week through this study.

DAY 1   *"Two people are better off than one, for they can help each other succeed. If one person falls, the other can reach out and help. But someone who falls alone is in real trouble. Likewise, two people lying close together can keep each other warm. But how can one be warm alone? A person standing alone can be attacked and defeated, but two can stand back-to-back and conquer. Three are even better, for a triple-braided cord is not easily broken." (Ecclesiastes 4:9–12 NLT)*

REFLECT: _____

_____

_____

_____

_____

_____

_____

_____

DAY 2   *"A man of many companions may come to ruin, but there is a friend who sticks closer than a brother." (Proverbs 18:24)*

REFLECT: _____

_____

_____

_____

_____

_____

_____

DAY 3   *"And Saul's son Jonathan went to David at Horesh and helped him find strength in God." (1 Samuel 23:16)*

REFLECT: _____

_____

_____

_____

_____

_____

_____

_____

_____

_____

_____

DAY 4   *"The LORD rewards every man for his righteousness and faithfulness. The LORD delivered you into my hands today, but I would not lay a hand on the LORD's anointed. As surely as I valued your life today, so may the LORD value my life and deliver me from all trouble." (1 Samuel 26:23 – 24)*

REFLECT: _____

_____

_____

_____

_____

_____

_____

_____

_____

_____

_____

DAY 5   *"A friend loves at all times, and a brother is born for adversity."*
(Proverbs 17:17)

REFLECT: _____

_____

_____

_____

_____

_____

_____

_____

_____

_____

_____

DAY 6   Use the following space to write any thoughts God has put in your
heart and mind about the things discussed during session one and/or
during your Reflections time this week.

SUMMARY: _____

_____

_____

_____

_____

_____

_____

_____

_____

_____

_____

RUTH AND NAOMI—
CONNECTED THROUGH LOSS

Remember when as kids we used to poke ourselves with a pin and press our fingers together to become blood brothers/sisters with our best friends? You didn't do this with just anybody. Becoming a blood brother/sister was serious business. It's a lot like family.

We should think of our relationships in Christ with at least this level of commitment. Blood brother/sisters look after each other. They don't let a little argument or disagreement get in the way of their relationship. Once you're in, there is no going back.

There was a sense that in pressing our fingers together, we were sharing each other's blood. Something of me went into you, and something of you came into me. We may not have thought this but it was intuitive, under the surface.

Even so, Christ has shared his blood with us through his death and resurrection. It is this that we commemorate whenever we share the Lord's Supper together. His blood not only washes us clean, it binds us together in his new covenant. Something of him is in us, and thus, in all of us, together. We are blood relatives with all other Christians. We should think of each other in this way.

CONNECTING WITH GOD'S FAMILY   20 MIN.

All kinds of situations may bring us together, but staying together, especially in our fast-paced, mobile society, is another matter. Families often live miles apart, friendships last from one job or one move to the next, and lasting marriages have become the exception rather than the rule. Still, we long for that permanent partnership—the one person who will love us unconditionally for all time. So when we read the story of Ruth and Naomi, we can't help but be drawn by their commitment to one another, deepened by grief, but bonded by the decision to stay together. In this session, we'll consider how God uses circumstances and choices to build lasting, lifetime friendships.

1. Pair up with your spiritual partner or, if your partner is absent, sit in with another pair for this question. Developing

27

friends in your neighborhood, church, or workplace is relatively easy. But imagine you were asked to live for a time outside your native culture and make friendships with people who don't even speak your language. If you were asked to do that right now, how would you likely respond? Check in with your spiritual partner. Share something God taught you during your time in his Word this week, or read a brief section from your journal. Be sure to write down your partner's progress on page 93.

2. Some of you in your group have been friends a long time. How did those friendships begin? Briefly share the story of how you first connected with someone in your group. Based on what that relationship means to you, what do you hope to get out of the next season in your life?

GROWING IN YOUR SPIRITUAL JOURNEY   40 MIN.

Ruth and Naomi's story reveals the deep level of love possible in relationships, even where there is no blood connection. In their case, it was a love that transcended cultural boundaries, marital traditions, troubled times, grief, and age differences—and ultimately changed history.

During a time of famine in the land, Naomi and her husband had left their native Bethlehem and moved to Moab. Miles from hearth and home, they slowly melded into their new culture. Then tragedy struck, and Naomi was widowed. Her two sons met and married Moabite brides, only to die as well. Now the three women, Naomi and her daughters-in-law, Orpah and Ruth, were left to provide for themselves. Where would they go? How would they live? Who would love them? The questions haunted Naomi's heart.

Too old to remarry, Naomi naturally longed to go back to Bethlehem where she had friends and family. But what would happen to Orpah and Ruth? In spite of their cultural differences, the three women loved each other deeply. Naomi urged the younger women to look after their own best interests—go, find new husbands, start new lives! But Ruth loved Naomi, and she loved hearing about Naomi's God. Ruth chose to stay with Naomi and convinced Naomi it was the right choice.

Because of a famine and a subsequent tragic loss, an ordinary Moabite woman with an extraordinary love was drawn to her mother-in-law's God and, in time, to a man named Boaz. Ultimately, Ruth would become the great-great-grandmother of King David and part of the lineage of Christ—all sparked by her lifetime commitment to her widowed mother-in-law. What legacy could your dedication to another potentially leave behind? It's something to think about.

Read Ruth 1:8–22:

Then Naomi said to her two daughters-in-law, "Go back, each of you, to your mother's home. May the LORD show kindness to you, as you have shown to your dead and to me. ⁹May the LORD grant that each of you will find rest in the home of another husband." Then she kissed them and they wept aloud ¹⁰and said to her, "We will go back with you to your people." ¹¹But Naomi said, "Return home, my daughters. Why would you come with me? Am I going to have any more sons, who could become your husbands? ¹²Return home, my daughters; I am too old to have another husband. Even if I thought there was still hope for me—even if I had a husband tonight and then gave birth to sons—¹³would you wait until they grew up? Would you remain unmarried for them? No, my daughters. It is more bitter for me than for you, because the LORD's hand has gone out against me!" ¹⁴At this they wept again. Then Orpah kissed her mother-in-law good-by, but Ruth clung to her. ¹⁵"Look," said Naomi, "your sister-in-law is going back to her people and her gods. Go back with her." ¹⁶But Ruth replied, "Don't urge me to leave you or to turn back from you. Where you go I will go, and where you stay I will stay. Your people will be my people and your God my God. ¹⁷Where you die I will die, and there I will be buried. May the LORD deal with me, be it ever so severely, if anything but death separates you and me." ¹⁸When Naomi realized that Ruth was determined to

go with her, she stopped urging her. ¹⁹*So the two women
went on until they came to Bethlehem. When they arrived
in Bethlehem, the whole town was stirred because of them,
and the women exclaimed, "Can this be Naomi?"* ²⁰*"Don't
call me Naomi," she told them. "Call me Mara, because the
Almighty has made my life very bitter.* ²¹*I went away full, but
the* LORD *has brought me back empty. Why call me Naomi?
The* LORD *has afflicted me; the Almighty has brought misfor-
tune upon me."* ²²*So Naomi returned from Moab accompa-
nied by Ruth the Moabitess, her daughter-in-law, arriving in
Bethlehem as the barley harvest was beginning.*

3. Ruth and Naomi's friendship developed through circum-
    stances in their lives—famine, marriage, death, and the
    need to go on in the face of tragedy. How do you think God
    uses circumstances to develop relationships in our lives?

4. How can even tragedy produce growth in our lives? If one or
    two of you have an experience of growth from grief—loss of
    a loved one, loss of finances, a broken relationship, or way-
    ward children—briefly share that story with your group.

5. Have someone in your group reread Ruth 1:11–13. Why do
    you think Naomi believed God's hand had come against her?

6. What perspective might have helped Naomi see her situation
    differently?

7. Ruth's story is a good example for us to consider today when friendships and acquaintances can be so fleeting. What do you think made Naomi willing, finally, to accept Ruth's commitment? If one or two of you are in a Naomi stage of life or have been a Ruth to someone else, share how God has used that relationship.

8. Why do you think Naomi speaks of her hardship in verses 20–21? How revealing should we be to one another of our own hardships?

9. In verse 16, what do you make of Ruth's willingness to embrace not only Naomi's people but her God? What does that say to you about our potential to influence another person's life for all eternity?

10. Name a few of the character qualities you see Ruth display in her relationship with Naomi. Why do you think God included this story in the Bible?

FOR DEEPER STUDY

Ruth is mentioned only one other time in Scripture outside the book that bears her name. Turn to Matthew 1:5. What do you discover about her there, and what does this say to you about the potential importance of our acts of faithfulness?

Ruth, Naomi, and Orpah all suffered devastating hardship. Yet God had a plan in which each of them would play a part. What do we read in Romans 8:28 that verifies their experiences, as well as those of each one of us as believers?

DEVELOPING YOUR GIFTS TO SERVE OTHERS   10 MIN.

11. On pages 96–97 you will find the Personal Health Assessment. Take a few minutes now to rate yourself in each area. You won't share your scores with the group. Plan to discuss with your spiritual partner one area where you are doing well and one area where you would like to grow. Everyone has areas in which they need to grow, so don't be discouraged or embarrassed. Note your findings on your Personal Health Plan on pages 92–93. Also record your next step for growth.

12. "Rotating Hosts and Leaders" is one of the group values we highly recommend for your group. People need opportunities to experiment with ways in which God may have gifted them. Your group will give you all the encouragement you need before, during, and after the session. Some groups like to let the host lead the meeting each week, while others like to let one person host while another person leads.

    The Small Group Calendar on page 91 is a tool for planning who will host and lead each meeting and who will provide refreshments. Take a few minutes to plan for your next four meetings. Don't pass this up! It will greatly impact your group.

SHARING YOUR LIFE MISSION EVERY DAY   10 MIN.

Today's world is filled with shallow relationships. A thirty-second viewing of almost any daytime television program is enough to see that is so.

13. Think about the person God led you to share with in session one, question 15. You are being an influence in that person's life — either for good or for bad. How can you show them that Christ makes a lasting difference?

14. Because of the loving, sacrificial witness of her life, Ruth came to love Naomi's God. Be like Naomi — don't keep

God to yourself. Ask yourself, "Who would benefit from this study?" and then plan to invite that person to your group next time. In order to identify those around you who might benefit from this study, use the following Circles of Life diagram to help you think about the people you come in contact with on a regular basis. Take a minute or two now to write down the names of those you know who have needs the group might be able to help meet.

CIRCLES OF LIFE

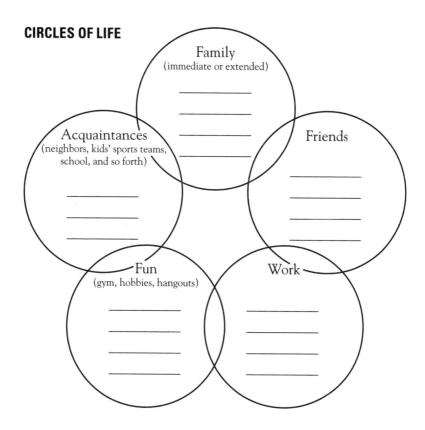

SURRENDERING YOUR LIFE FOR GOD'S PLEASURE   15 – 20 MIN.

Submitting our lives to another is not always about what we want or who we want to be with. As believers, God asks us in Ephesians 5:21 to "be subject to one another in the fear of Christ" (NASB). As a group, read Ruth 1:16 – 17 aloud together:

But Ruth replied, "Don't urge me to leave you or to turn back from you. Where you go I will go, and where you stay I will stay. Your people will be my people and your God my God. [17]Where you die I will die, and there I will be buried. May the LORD deal with me, be it ever so severely, if anything but death separates you and me."

15. Now, as a group, turn these words into a prayer of commitment to God. Say, "Lord, where you send us, we will go. Where you ask us to stay, we will stay. Your people are our people, and you are our God. How grateful we are for the gift of your Son, through whose sacrifice we can know that not even death can separate us from your love."

Or write your own prayer here:

16. Be sure to use the Prayer and Praise Report on page 35 to record each others' prayer requests.

STUDY NOTES

Go back. Naomi encourages her daughters-in-law to return to their mother's quarters in preparation for another marriage. This is another way of saying, "God will honor your commitment to me by giving you a new life."

The LORD's hand has gone out against me! This is a common expression for "God is working." It is seen not as a harsh affliction but the activity of the Lord in our lives — God's "overruling activity," as the *New International Bible Commentary* puts it. See also Ruth 1:20 where Naomi (meaning "pleasant") changed her name to Mara (meaning "bitter"). Hardship and affliction bring about a sobering of one's perspective — the goal for the Christian is to become better, not bitter.

Clung. This is a translation of the Hebrew word *dabaq*, meaning "to follow close (hard after), to be joined (together)." Commitment is evidenced by closeness in proximity.

Briefly share your prayer requests with the large group, making notations below.
Then gather in small groups of two to four to pray for each other.

Date: _____

PRAYER REQUESTS

_____

_____

_____

_____

_____

_____

_____

_____

_____

_____

_____

PRAISE REPORT

_____

_____

_____

_____

_____

_____

_____

_____

_____

REFLECTIONS

Each day read the daily verse(s) and give prayerful consideration to what you learn about God, his Spirit, and his place in your life. Then record your thoughts, insights, or prayer in the Reflect section. On day six record a summary of what you have learned over the entire week through this study.

DAY 1   *"Submit to one another out of reverence for Christ." (Ephesians 5:21)*

REFLECT: _____

_____

_____

_____

_____

_____

_____

_____

_____

DAY 2   *"Be devoted to one another in brotherly love. Honor one another above yourselves." (Romans 12:10)*

REFLECT: _____

_____

_____

_____

_____

_____

_____

_____

DAY 3   *"And we know that God causes all things to work together for good to those who love God, to those who are called according to His purpose." (Romans 8:28 NASB)*

REFLECT: _____

_____

_____

_____

_____

_____

_____

_____

_____

_____

DAY 4   *" 'For my thoughts are not your thoughts, neither are your ways my ways,' declares the LORD. 'As the heavens are higher than the earth, so are my ways higher than your ways and my thoughts than your thoughts.' " (Isaiah 55:8–9)*

REFLECT: _____

_____

_____

_____

_____

_____

_____

_____

_____

_____

_____

DAY 5   *"For as high as the heavens are above the earth, so great is his love for those who fear him." (Psalm 103:11)*

REFLECT: _____

_____

_____

_____

_____

_____

_____

_____

_____

_____

_____

DAY 6   Use the following space to write any thoughts God has put in your heart and mind about the things discussed during session two and/or during your Reflections time this week.

SUMMARY: _____

_____

_____

_____

_____

_____

_____

_____

_____

_____

_____

JESUS AND PETER — FAITHFUL FRIENDS

Upon completing the last match of his illustrious career in August of 2006, Andre Agassi made a comment that went way beyond just his experience as a professional tennis player. It was a comment with profound application to our experience of truth and how we come to a deeper understanding of God and his will for our lives. "The scoreboard says I lost today," Agassi told the adoring crowd that had come to see his final match, "but what the scoreboard doesn't say is what it is that I have found."

It's always been a major principle in God's economy. You lose so you can find. I lost my keys yesterday only to find the book I've been missing for weeks in the process of looking for my keys. I lost my job only to find out that God had a much better position waiting for me somewhere else. I lost my girlfriend only to find my wife. I lost my sight, but now I can see in ways I never thought possible. I lost the race, but I gained a new friend among the losers.

A woman lost her pride and her expensive perfume at the feet of Jesus, from whom she found forgiveness and eternal life. Peter lost his dignity and his reputation among the other disciples, but he gained his forgiveness and a deeper relationship with his Lord.

"The scoreboard says that I lost today, but what the scoreboard doesn't say is what it is that I have found." The end of this is simple: Don't pay too much attention to the score; just keep a sharp eye out for what God is teaching you in the process of living.

CONNECTING WITH GOD'S FAMILY   20 MIN.

Today's headlines are filled with stories of betrayal — whether it's a wife suing an ex-husband, a politician breaking a campaign promise, or a corporate executive accused of fraud. Does loyalty really matter anymore? Repeatedly, polls and surveys reflect the unraveling of our ethical fiber.

Yet we long for faithful relationships. We often spend years searching for that one person who won't let us down. Jesus modeled a friendship like that with Peter. In this lesson, we'll examine loyalty as revealed in their relationship.

1. Have you ever known someone who said one thing, but did another? One or two of you share how that example influenced your life.

2. Pair up with your spiritual partner or, if your partner is absent, sit in with another pair for this question. Would you consider yourself a loyal person? If so, why? Then, check in with your spiritual partner and share what have you been learning from God recently.

GROWING IN YOUR SPIRITUAL JOURNEY   40 MIN.

"Simon son of John," Jesus began. Peter knew the Lord was getting serious. What happened to calling him "Peter"? Couldn't they just enjoy the after-dinner warmth from the fire and continue to revel in the fact that Jesus was back from the dead? Why did he have to get serious?

"Do you truly love me more than these?" Jesus asked.

Oh no, Peter squirmed. Why did he keep asking, "Do you love me unconditionally?" Twice now, he'd used that Greek word *agape*, the one Peter did not like. *Agape*—such a serious word!

"Yes, Lord, you *know* that I love you," Peter answered, but he couldn't quite bring himself to say *agape*. *Phileo*—that word for brotherly love meant almost the same thing, didn't it? Peter could do *phileo*. He wasn't so sure about *agape*.

"Feed my lambs," Jesus kept saying.

"Are you even my friend, Peter?" That one stung.

Three times now Jesus had asked him if he loved him and Peter had answered him—three times. Three times Jesus said, "Feed my sheep." What was up with this? What did he mean? He must still be angry about that denial.

Oh, Peter thought. *I get it! Jesus is going away again—this time for good. He needs someone to take care of his disciples, someone to feed his young church, someone he can trust to do the right thing. That must mean he's forgiven me!*

Peter had messed up in the past, but Jesus knew his heart. He knew that in Peter he had a loyal follower—a faithful friend who would care for his sheep.

Now Jesus was saying something else—something about a day in the future when someone would lead Peter where he didn't want to go. Why did he have to get so serious? But Peter loved him. Yes, he decided. He would follow Jesus anywhere—and he would feed his sheep.

Read John 21:15–19:

> *When they had finished eating, Jesus said to Simon Peter, "Simon son of John, do you truly love me more than these?" "Yes, Lord," he said, "you know that I love you." Jesus said, "Feed my lambs." ¹⁶Again Jesus said, "Simon son of John, do you truly love me?" He answered, "Yes, Lord, you know that I love you." Jesus said, "Take care of my sheep." ¹⁷The third time he said to him, "Simon son of John, do you love me?" Peter was hurt because Jesus asked him the third time, "Do you love me?" He said, "Lord, you know all things; you know that I love you." ¹⁸Jesus said, "Feed my sheep. I tell you the truth, when you were younger you dressed yourself and went where you wanted; but when you are old you will stretch out your hands, and someone else will dress you and lead you where you do not want to go." ¹⁹Jesus said this to indicate the kind of death by which Peter would glorify God. Then he said to him, "Follow me!"*

3. Jesus' repeated questioning of Peter's love and loyalty to him (John 21:15–17) wounded Peter, but Jesus had a purpose in his persistence. What previous experience in Peter's life do you think Jesus is clarifying by asking three times if he loved him? Look at John 13:36–38.

4. What do you think you would say if Jesus asked you the same thing he asked Peter? Do you truly love Jesus?

5. Do actions always prove we mean what we say? Explain.

6. In the verses from John 21, Jesus was appearing to Peter in his resurrected form — a sight that must have stunned Peter and helped root his faith. Everything Jesus had told him was true! Now, the man he spoke with was not just his friend and master, but his risen Lord. How do you think you would respond if Christ were to appear right now in your living room and ask you this same question: "Do you love me?"

7. Jesus draws a direct relationship between the questions, "Do you love me?" and the directions, "Feed my sheep." Through his obedient response, Peter went on to become a history-changing influence for Christ, demonstrating his love for Jesus through his powerful ministry. What are some of the ways we can show our love for Jesus by feeding his sheep? Look at John 12:3–8; Matthew 10:42; 21:6–7.

8. What does "feed my sheep" mean to you? How does "feed my sheep" differ from "tend my sheep"? (See Study Notes.)

9. For Peter to hear Jesus address the disciple's own future martyrdom (John 21:19) certainly had to challenge his decision to follow Christ. What might be the greatest challenge facing you as you consider following after Christ, knowing

the possible affliction that awaits you (see Matthew 19:29)? What does this say about Peter's friendship with Jesus?

FOR DEEPER STUDY

In John 13:36–38, Jesus warns Peter he will deny Jesus three times before morning. Peter, of course, vigorously denied he would do such a thing. Look now at Mark 14:66–72. How did Peter respond when he realized he had indeed denied his Master?

Compare Peter's response to that of Judas, who betrayed Christ (see Matthew 27:3–5). Which do you think shows true repentance? Consider genuine repentance as a component of loyalty.

According to John 13:38, what did Jesus understand about Peter that Peter could not yet see? Have you ever had that kind of insight into someone you loved, one that enabled you to understand their potential response to a circumstance better than they themselves understood it? How did you handle that situation?

What did God teach you as a result?

DEVELOPING YOUR GIFTS TO SERVE OTHERS　　　10 MIN.

You don't have to be a pastor or a "professional" Christian to hear Jesus' call to feed his sheep—which can mean anything from nourishing others with his Word to simply responding to the needs around us as he reveals them. Feeding his sheep can take on a variety of different forms, and the body of Christ needs them all. It's why he's given us so many different gifts and abilities. Through them, he asks this of each one of us: "Feed my sheep."

10. Who in your life is Jesus asking you to shepherd? Plan what you will do to feed those sheep (or that lamb) this week. It could be as simple as an encouraging letter or phone call, or an invitation to a Bible study at your church. Investing in the lives of others is being like Christ.

    Who is a shepherd in your life? If you're not sure of the answer, ask God to begin revealing that person to you or to bring someone alongside to shepherd you. Write their name here and make a plan for doing this:

    _____

SHARING YOUR LIFE MISSION EVERY DAY　　　10 MIN.

11. When we think of feeding sheep, our minds typically jump to members of the church. But sheep often come from outside the church. Paul, in fact, is an example of a sheep who started out life as a wolf to Christians! How could your example reach a Paul you know? Who is a sheep outside the walls of the church you could feed?

12. Groups that focus outwardly grow much deeper in their relationships than those that look only inward. Return to the Circles of Life diagram on page 33 and look at the names of those you chose to invite to this group. How did it go? Do you still need to follow up?

13. Jesus wanted Peter to understand that loving him meant more than going on occasional walks or hanging out with him as he taught. Loving him is a lifetime commitment. Are you ready to say to him, "Yes, Lord"? What changes will this make in your life daily?

14. As a group, join hands and imagine that Jesus is standing before you (his Word clearly says that wherever two or more are gathered, he is in their midst — Matthew 18:20), asking you the same questions he asked of Peter all those years ago. How will you answer when he says to you,

   "[YOUR NAME], do you truly love me more than these?"

   "[YOUR NAME], do you truly love me?"

   "[YOUR NAME], do you love me?"

15. Is there anyone in your life to whom you are confessing love and commitment — but failing to back up your words with action? As God reveals that name to your heart, write it here. Confess your past failure to demonstrate true love and loyalty as you ask God's help to take action.

   _____ *(Write name here)*

16. Break into groups of two or three to share your prayer requests and pray for one another. Record any requests or praises on the Prayer and Praise Report on page 47.

STUDY NOTES

Do you love me? Notice that Jesus uses both *agape* love (unconditional love) and *phileo* love (friendship love). Jesus is not asking Peter if he loves the sheep but if Peter loves Jesus. Twice he asks about *agape* love and once about *phileo*. Jesus is not simply asking about Peter's unconditional loyalty but his friendship. He brought into question the basis of their friendship. Love is friendship as much as it is unconditional.

Feed/tend. The words are used interchangeably and refer to the nurture and concern a shepherd has for his flock. Jesus refers to his people as *lambs* and *sheep*. A lamb is a reference to a younger sheep. Sheep are older, those that have walked on in years. According to *The Gospel According to St. John* by B. F. Westcott, "The lambs require to be fed; the sheep require to be guided." There is a greater responsibility to the mature Christian to not only feed but also raise up, train, and release God's flock.

Hurt. Sorrow and heaviness gripped Peter's heart. He knew his ability to serve Christ was based on the depth of his commitment. He knew it had been less than adequate for the task laid before him. Where would he come up with this kind of love? The answer lies in Jesus' challenge to Peter in verse 19.

Briefly share your prayer requests with the large group, making notations below. Then gather in small groups of two to four to pray for each other.

Date: _____

PRAYER REQUESTS

_____

_____

_____

_____

_____

_____

_____

_____

_____

_____

_____

PRAISE REPORT

_____

_____

_____

_____

_____

_____

_____

_____

REFLECTIONS

Each day read the daily verse(s) and give prayerful consideration to what you learn about God, his Spirit, and his place in your life. Then record your thoughts, insights, or prayer in the Reflect section. On day six record a summary of what you have learned over the entire week through this study.

DAY 1   *"Let love and faithfulness never leave you; bind them around your neck, write them on the tablet of your heart. Then you will win favor and a good name in the sight of God and man."* (Proverbs 3:3–4)

REFLECT: _____

_____

_____

_____

_____

_____

DAY 2   *"When they had finished eating, Jesus said to Simon Peter, 'Simon son of John, do you truly love me more than these?' 'Yes, Lord,' he said, 'you know that I love you.' Jesus said, 'Feed my lambs.' Again Jesus said, 'Simon son of John, do you truly love me?' He answered, 'Yes, Lord, you know that I love you.' Jesus said, 'Take care of my sheep.' The third time he said to him, 'Simon son of John, do you love me?' Peter was hurt because Jesus asked him the third time, 'Do you love me?' He said, 'Lord, you know all things; you know that I love you.'"* (John 21:15–17)

REFLECT: _____

_____

_____

_____

_____

DAY 3   *"Peter asked, 'Lord, why can't I follow you now? I will lay down my life for you.' Then Jesus answered, 'Will you really lay down your life for me? I tell you the truth, before the rooster crows, you will disown me three times.'" (John 13:37–38)*

REFLECT: _____

_____

_____

_____

_____

_____

_____

_____

_____

_____

_____

_____

DAY 4   *"And if anyone gives even a cup of cold water to one of these little ones because he is my disciple, I tell you the truth, he will certainly not lose his reward." (Matthew 10:42)*

REFLECT: _____

_____

_____

_____

_____

_____

_____

_____

_____

_____

_____

_____

_____

_____

DAY 5   *"And everyone who has left houses or brothers or sisters or father or mother or children or fields for my sake will receive a hundred times as much and will inherit eternal life." (Matthew 19:29)*

REFLECT: _____

_____

_____

_____

_____

_____

_____

_____

_____

_____

_____

_____

DAY 6   *Use the following space to write any thoughts God has put in your heart and mind about the things discussed during session three and/ or during your Reflections time this week.*

SUMMARY: _____

_____

_____

_____

_____

_____

_____

_____

_____

_____

_____

_____

PHILIP AND THE EUNUCH — INTERRUPTED FOR GOD

Once on a three-hour flight, in seat 11B, I found myself trapped between a beautiful woman in 11A and a man in 11C who wished he could get closer to the woman in 11A. So either I was going to exchange seats with the man, let him talk over me, or wake up in the middle of this thing and join the conversation, which is what I reluctantly decided to do.

In the process of this flight, I came up with two important conclusions: (1) Be a knowledgeable person. Have something to talk about. It's a big world, and the Lord is the Lord of it all. If Jesus is the way, the truth, and the life, you should be able to start anywhere and end up with him. (2) Don't tell people you're a Christian too soon; they might just happen to like you. And then when you finally do tell them you're a Christian, they might decide to like you anyway, which, in this case, was what they did. And for three hours, we covered numerous subjects, the most interesting one being my faith, which they were both extremely curious about.

By the time we landed I had told these two everything about the gospel I could ever want to say, yet none of it was forced, planned, rehearsed, or manipulated. They had actually pulled it out of me! I just fastened my seatbelt, jumped into the conversation, and held on for the ride. Sometimes that's the best witness you can be.

CONNECTING WITH GOD'S FAMILY   20 MIN.

Friendships often find us where we least expect them — sometimes when we're not looking for them at all. They can be for a lifetime, or just for a season, as we read in the story of Philip and the Ethiopian eunuch. Because he was willing to befriend a stranger for God, Philip introduced this man — an important national official — to his savior, Jesus Christ. The Bible tells us the eunuch was saved as a result. History tells us Ethiopia became a Christian nation — all because one man, Philip, sought God's agenda rather than his own.

1. Have you ever been interrupted by "a feeling" you were supposed to talk with someone who was a total stranger? What happened when you felt that prompting?

2. Pair up with your spiritual partner or, if your partner is absent, sit in with another pair for this question: What have you discovered about being or finding a shepherd since your last session? Then, check in with your spiritual partner. What have you been learning from God during your personal time with him?

GROWING IN YOUR SPIRITUAL JOURNEY   40 MIN.

Back in Samaria, Philip had a booming ministry going (see Acts 8:5–8). Miracles were happening, people were rejoicing— God and Philip were popular in Samaria. At the top of his game, Philip was suddenly asked by God to leave it all behind and set out on a lonely trip, on a desert road from Jerusalem to Gaza. Leave now? When everything was going so well? But Philip did not question God—he simply obeyed.

Before long, Philip came upon a man traveling back to Ethiopia from Jerusalem, where he had gone to worship God. Philip responded by approaching the eunuch. He asked the man if he understood what he was reading. The eunuch welcomed his help. At this point, Philip could have shown off his knowledge of Scripture by taking him back to Genesis, but instead he wisely met the man exactly where he was.

Philip's obedience met God's perfect timing and the man gave his heart to Christ. Using his influential role, the man began spreading the gospel message within a new culture—an example of taking the gospel "to the uttermost parts of the earth." Some friendships are meant for a lifetime and some are just for a window in time. What matters, as Philip teaches us, is our obedient response to God's Spirit.

Read Acts 8:26–39:

Now an angel of the Lord said to Philip, "Go south to the road—the desert road—that goes down from Jerusalem to Gaza." ²⁷So he started out, and on his way he met an Ethiopian eunuch, an important official in charge of all the treasury of Candace, queen of the Ethiopians. This man had gone to Jerusalem to worship, ²⁸and on his way home was sitting in his chariot reading the book of Isaiah the prophet. ²⁹The Spirit told Philip, "Go to that chariot and stay near it."

³⁰Then Philip ran up to the chariot and heard the man reading Isaiah the prophet. "Do you understand what you are reading?" Philip asked. ³¹"How can I," he said, "unless someone explains it to me?" So he invited Philip to come up and sit with him. ³²The eunuch was reading this passage of Scripture: "He was led like a sheep to the slaughter, and as a lamb before the shearer is silent, so he did not open his mouth. ³³In his humiliation he was deprived of justice. Who can speak of his descendants? For his life was taken from the earth." ³⁴The eunuch asked Philip, "Tell me, please, who is the prophet talking about, himself or someone else?" ³⁵Then Philip began with that very passage of Scripture and told him the good news about Jesus. ³⁶As they traveled along the road, they came to some water and the eunuch said, "Look, here is water. Why shouldn't I be baptized?" ³⁸And he gave orders to stop the chariot. Then both Philip and the eunuch went down into the water and Philip baptized him. ³⁹When they came up out of the water, the Spirit of the Lord suddenly took Philip away, and the eunuch did not see him again, but went on his way rejoicing.

3. Opportunity is often found where we least expect it, as Philip discovered. Has God ever stopped you in your tracks— maybe at an inconvenient moment—and presented you with an opportunity? Share the incident briefly with the group.

4. Why do you think it is so hard for us in today's world to recognize opportunities from God to connect with others? Offer ideas for learning to hear God's voice more clearly.

5. Philip's willingness to go where God sent him, in spite of the interruption in his personal plans, speaks to us about the need to be open for God's leading. Where could God use your willing response to make a difference for others?

6. Considering society's current climate, it might seem unexpected for a government official to positively respond to the gospel message. What can each of us do to be a Christlike influence on our government officials?

7. Philip could have shared Christ with this man differently. He chose to meet him where he was. How can we follow this example when God presents us with opportunities for friendship evangelism?

8. Have someone read Colossians 4:2–6. What does God want from each of us?

FOR DEEPER STUDY

By sharing Christ with the Ethiopian eunuch, how was Philip helping to fulfill prophecy? See Isaiah 56:2–5.

Think about the lesson of Philip and the Ethiopian eunuch and the message from Isaiah and answer this question: Since only God ultimately knows who will and who will not receive Christ, how do you think we should regard everyone else, whether or not he or she is a believer in this moment?

DEVELOPING YOUR GIFTS TO SERVE OTHERS   10 MIN.

Philip was a gifted preacher whose openness to share the gospel with others clearly changed many lives. What are you especially good at? You don't need to be a preacher to change people's lives.

9. Make a list of the things you do best and ask God to show you how to use those special abilities to bless others for his sake. Share one of those things with your group and invite them to offer ideas.

10. As a group, evaluate the strengths you have within your group. How are you suited to reach out together and touch the lives of those within the church or in your community?

11. Take a few minutes to discuss the future of this group. How many of you are willing to stay together and work through another study? If you have time, turn to the Small Group

Agreement on pages 89–90 and talk about any changes you would like to make as you move forward.

SHARING YOUR LIFE MISSION EVERY DAY   10 MIN.

12. Unlike the other biblical characters we have studied so far in this series, Philip and the Ethiopian eunuch were not friends at the outset. Do you think they became friends as a result of this encounter? Explain your answer. How could God use your willingness to share with "outsiders" as an opportunity to cultivate potentially life-changing friendships?

13. Would you be able to explain to a nonbeliever a passage of Scripture they were reading, as Philip did for the Ethiopian man? What step could you take this week to make sure you are ready for such a time as this?

SURRENDERING YOUR LIFE FOR GOD'S PLEASURE   15–20 MIN.

14. When it comes to living a surrendered life, there are few examples in Scripture greater than the one Philip presents in this passage. As a group, read again Acts 8:26–30, focusing on Philip's response to the angel's/Spirit's instructions. Then read John 15:13. Ask God to help you be ready at all times to do what he asks you to do on behalf of another. Pray for friends in whose lives you can make an eternal difference, as Philip did.

15. Share your prayer requests and record them on the Prayer and Praise Report on page 58. Then spend a few minutes praying for them. Don't forget to pray for these throughout the week.

STUDY NOTES

Angel of the Lord. Angels lead, faithful men and women follow, and God supplies the details. Other examples include: Hagar (Genesis 16:7–13); Abraham (Genesis 22:11–14); Moses (Exodus 3:2); Balaam (Numbers 22:22–35). This is often a reference to any special or direct activity of the Lord.

Ethiopian eunuch. Based on his title, "a court official of Candace," this man was a servant of a ruler much like a caesar or a pharaoh. We know he was dedicated to the Scriptures and was probably a Gentile convert to Judaism. The question lies in whether "eunuch" describes him as a government official from the Orient or an emasculated male or maybe both. As a possible physical eunuch, he would have been denied access to the temple and becoming a full proselyte to Judaism (Deuteronomy 23:1). The text makes him out to be a seeker at heart, religious but not yet a follower of Jesus.

Go to that chariot and stay near it. The command would have been difficult for Philip to receive and obey. Think of all the differences between Philip and the Ethiopian eunuch—racially, religiously, socioeconomically. Yet Philip obeyed and went to this man.

Told him the good news about Jesus. Literally, "he preached Jesus to him." When the opportunity is right, take it. This man was reading from Isaiah 53:7–8. Take a look at Isaiah 56:6–8. If the eunuch had kept reading, he would have read of God's grace given to all.

Philip baptized him. Water baptism follows conversion. See Matthew 28:18–20.

Briefly share your prayer requests with the large group, making notations below. Then gather in small groups of two to four to pray for each other.

Date: _____

PRAYER REQUESTS

_____

_____

_____

_____

_____

_____

_____

_____

_____

_____

_____

_____

PRAISE REPORT

_____

_____

_____

_____

_____

_____

_____

_____

REFLECTIONS

Each day read the daily verse(s) and give prayerful consideration to what you learn about God, his Spirit, and his place in your life. Then record your thoughts, insights, or prayer in the Reflect section. On day six record a summary of what you have learned over the entire week through this study.

DAY 1 *"Now an angel of the Lord said to Philip, 'Go south to the road—the desert road—that goes down from Jerusalem to Gaza.' So he started out, and on his way he met an Ethiopian eunuch, an important official in charge of all the treasury of Candace, queen of the Ethiopians. This man had gone to Jerusalem to worship, and on his way home was sitting in his chariot reading the book of Isaiah the prophet. The Spirit told Philip, 'Go to that chariot and stay near it.'"* (Acts 8:26–29)

REFLECT: _____

_____

_____

_____

_____

_____

_____

DAY 2 *"Then Philip ran up to the chariot and heard the man reading Isaiah the prophet. 'Do you understand what you are reading?' Philip asked. 'How can I,' he said, 'unless someone explains it to me?' So he invited Philip to come up and sit with him."* (Acts 8:30–31)

REFLECT: _____

_____

_____

_____

_____

_____

_____

DAY 3   *"But in your hearts set apart Christ as Lord. Always be prepared to give an answer to everyone who asks you to give the reason for the hope that you have. But do this with gentleness and respect." (1 Peter 3:15)*

REFLECT: _____

_____

_____

_____

_____

_____

_____

_____

_____

_____

DAY 4   *"Devote yourselves to prayer, being watchful and thankful. And pray for us, too, that God may open a door for our message, so that we may proclaim the mystery of Christ, for which I am in chains. Pray that I may proclaim it clearly, as I should." (Colossians 4:2–4)*

REFLECT: _____

_____

_____

_____

_____

_____

_____

_____

_____

_____

DAY 5   *"Be wise in the way you act toward outsiders; make the most of every opportunity. Let your conversation be always full of grace, seasoned with salt, so that you may know how to answer everyone."* (Colossians 4:5–6)

REFLECT: _____

_____

_____

_____

_____

_____

_____

_____

_____

_____

_____

DAY 6   Use the following space to write any thoughts God has put in your heart and mind about the things discussed during session four and/or during your Reflections time this week.

SUMMARY: _____

_____

_____

_____

_____

_____

_____

_____

_____

_____

_____

PAUL AND BARNABAS — CONFLICT MANAGEMENT

Once, as a visitor on a Christian college campus, I got into a conflict with a dean in the administration. Later, in a letter to the school paper, he used that forum to strike as many blows against me as he could. Weeks later, someone sent me the article, and for a while I carried it around and read it to my friends as we all shook our heads at how narrow-minded and bigoted this man could be.

It wasn't long until I began to feel sick to my stomach. The Holy Spirit was helping me realize that whatever he had done to me, however bad it might have been, did not give me an excuse to return the favor. On just my side of the equation — the only part I'm responsible for — I was blowing it. So I confessed my sin to the Lord and tore up the article. But the Lord didn't let me stop there. He kept pressing me until I realized he wanted me to go find the man and ask forgiveness for slandering him before my friends. That was quite a step for me, since I was so convinced of the magnitude of *his* error, I could barely see mine.

So I made an appointment, met the man, and in the process of talking, I found out that he had had a terrible year culminating in the loss of his wife to cancer. For some reason, my seeking him out and confessing my sin to him opened his heart to me, and we ended up laughing, and crying, and praying for each other, forgetting even the nature of our differences. It's amazing what the Holy Spirit can do if we walk into a conflict, convinced of our wrong-doing and seeking to make it right.

CONNECTING WITH GOD'S FAMILY   20 MIN.

Conflicts are inevitable in life — even among Christians. How can we "agree to disagree agreeably," or resolve our conflicts without tearing apart our friendships? Most of us have known the pain of at least one broken relationship. In this session, we'll peek in on the clash between Paul and his good friend Barnabas over young John Mark. We'll talk about what caused their division and how God ultimately brought them back together.

1. Check in with your spiritual partner. Share how you were able to respond to God's leading to meet a need when it wasn't convenient this past week. What was the result?

2. Have you ever felt strongly that someone should be included in your circle of friendships or work environment, in spite of opposition from others? Explain.

GROWING IN YOUR SPIRITUAL JOURNEY   40 MIN.

Though brothers on the battlefield of Christ, Paul and Barnabas didn't exactly see eye to eye when it came to young John Mark. Because John Mark had deserted them during an earlier campaign, Paul had trouble trusting the young man's commitment. The argument was intense enough to cause a division between Paul and Barnabas, who went their separate ways for a while.

While it is not known for certain, many scholars believe John Mark is the young man who fled in fear when Jesus was arrested, leaving his clothes behind. In spite of his early tendencies to "cut and run," John Mark went on, thanks to Barnabas's patient discipling, to become a trusted companion to three Christian leaders—Barnabas, Paul, and Peter—and one of the first to actually record a gospel account (the gospel according to Mark).

Read Acts 15:36–41:

> Some time later Paul said to Barnabas, "Let us go back and visit the brothers in all the towns where we preached the word of the Lord and see how they are doing." 37Barnabas wanted to take John, also called Mark, with them, 38but Paul did not think it wise to take him, because he had deserted them in Pamphylia and had not continued with them in the work. 39They had such a sharp disagreement that they parted company. Barnabas took Mark and sailed for Cyprus, 40but Paul chose Silas and left, commended by the brothers to the grace of the Lord.

41He went through Syria and Cilicia, strengthening the churches.

3. Before they quarreled over John Mark, Paul asked Barnabas to accompany him on a mission to revisit the believers in all the towns where they had previously preached the gospel (see Acts 15:36). What part do you think this plan may have ultimately played in the spiritual growth of the early church?

4. Why was Paul suspicious of John Mark? (See Acts 15:38.)

5. Barnabas saw potential in John Mark that Paul could not yet see. Considering the fact that John Mark later became a valued ministry partner (see Colossians 4:10; 2 Timothy 4:11), what do you think Barnabas understood about the nature of mistakes?

6. If you were a missionary-in-training, as John Mark was, whose mentorship would you rather be under — Paul's or Barnabas's? It's easy to think Paul was being too stern, but could he have been right to have misgivings about John Mark?

7. It's amazing to note that in spite of the first apostles' personal imperfections and failure to always model Christ before one another, God grew this early church into what we are today. How does John Mark's story encourage us to be patient with ourselves and others as we grow in Christ?

8. Is there someone in your life with whom you disagree, though you recognize you are both attempting to serve the Lord? If your disagreement is holding you back from serving, what would help you learn to accept your differences and move on?

FOR DEEPER STUDY

There is an old saying that wherever there are two believers, there are often three opinions, "Yours, mine, and the Holy Spirit's." Only one is right! The argument between Paul and Barnabas stands out as an early example of this situation. When we are caught in conflict with another Christian, how can we make it our personal goal to work through the disagreement with minimal emotional damage? Is it always possible to do this? (You might wonder, is it *ever* possible?) Share some ideas or a success story if you have one. For more on conflict resolution, study Jesus' teaching in Matthew 18:15–19.

What is the first thing Jesus says we should do when we feel a brother or sister in Christ has offended us (Matthew 18:15)?

How do we tend to actually handle these situations and what often happens as a result?

Over and over as we encounter the teaching of Jesus, we find he calls us to live differently from others in the world: "But among you it will be different. Whoever wants to be a leader among you must be your servant" (Matthew 20:26 NLT). What will you do the next time you face conflict with another believer, in order to make sure that, for your part, you are obeying Christ?

DEVELOPING YOUR GIFTS TO SERVE OTHERS   10 MIN.

9. We also discover from the book of Acts that Barnabas had the spiritual gift of encouragement. Over time, his encouragement won John Mark back into the fold so that eventually the young man became a trusted coworker with Paul (Colossians 4:10; 2 Timothy 4:11; Philemon 24). Peter even called John Mark his son (1 Peter 5:13). How do you think God wants to use your giftedness to grow the body of Christ and strengthen the bond of love Christ longs for us to know and show to the world around us?

10. Is there someone God might want you to mentor for him, as Barnabas did with John Mark? Write that person's name here and ask the group to pray with you for both patience and creativity in guiding that spiritually young believer.

My John Mark is_____

11. Take a moment or two in your group to affirm one another's differences, praising God for his love of variety and desire to use each one of us uniquely for his kingdom. Why not use those gifts to minister right in your group? If you have Barnabas's gift, encourage someone who is struggling. Maybe you have the gift of hospitality. Organize and host a celebration party at the end of this study. If exhortation or teaching

is your gift, consider leading your group for the next month. God longs to develop the gifts he has given us, and through our groups he's given us a community in which to do so.

SHARING YOUR LIFE MISSION EVERY DAY   10 MIN.

12. It's easy to look down on John Mark for his early fear, but the truth is, sharing the gospel is scary! Mysterious as it seems, the truth is, people are rarely excited to hear this good news—at least, not *before* they've heard it! When it comes to telling others about Christ, are you a Paul or a John Mark? Obviously, we don't all have the gift of evangelism. In addition to verbally sharing the gospel, what are some other ways we can share Christ? Offer a few suggestions. Remember that God wants to use us just the way he made us.

SURRENDERING YOUR LIFE FOR GOD'S PLEASURE   15–20 MIN.

13. If you are currently experiencing a Paul and Barnabas-like conflict over another individual or issue, ask your group to pray for you to have a right heart before God on this matter.

14. As a group, pray for God to help you make a difference in the lives of new believers, who may have many questions about the Christian life, as well as in all whose lives you touch. If any of you *are* new believers like John Mark once was, it's our prayer for you that this group will be a safe place to grow.

15. Look ahead to question 12 of the Surrendering section on page 79 in session six. You will have the opportunity to celebrate the work God is doing in each of you through a time of Communion together—if you decide it is appropriate for your group. The instructions for serving Communion are on pages 98–99 of the appendix. Plan who will provide everything that is needed to make this a meaningful occasion.

STUDY NOTES

Paul and Barnabas. Both were apostles of the early church. Paul had converted from Judaism to Christianity later in his life when he met the Lord on the road to Damascus (Acts 9). Barnabas was also a Jewish convert. Acts 4:36–37 describes Barnabas as a giver (he sold some land to give money to the poor). His name means "son of consolation" or encourager.

Deserted them. Later Paul and Barnabas would be described as colleagues (1 Corinthians 9:6) which seems to allude to the fact that they worked out their differences about Mark. Though Mark once deserted the mission field, various Scriptures indicate he faithfully completed his missionary charge.

Sharp disagreement. Luke is honest about Paul and Barnabas's conflict but also reveals how this disagreement was used to expand the missionary efforts. The language does not infer irreconcilable differences but merely a difference in perspective.

PRAYER AND PRAISE REPORT

Briefly share your prayer requests with the large group, making notations below. Then gather in small groups of two to four to pray for each other.

Date: _____

PRAYER REQUESTS

_____
_____
_____
_____
_____
_____
_____
_____
_____
_____
_____
_____

PRAISE REPORT

_____
_____
_____
_____
_____
_____
_____
_____
_____

REFLECTIONS

Each day read the daily verse(s) and give prayerful consideration to what you learn about God, his Spirit, and his place in your life. Then record your thoughts, insights, or prayer in the Reflect section. On day six record a summary of what you have learned over the entire week through this study.

DAY 1   *"If your brother sins against you, go and show him his fault, just between the two of you. If he listens to you, you have won your brother over. But if he will not listen, take one or two others along, so that 'every matter may be established by the testimony of two or three witnesses.' If he refuses to listen to them, tell it to the church; and if he refuses to listen even to the church, treat him as you would a pagan or a tax collector." (Matthew 18:15 – 17)*

REFLECT: _____

_____

_____

_____

_____

_____

_____

_____

DAY 2   *"But among you it will be different. Whoever wants to be a leader among you must be your servant." (Matthew 20:26 NLT)*

REFLECT: _____

_____

_____

_____

_____

_____

_____

_____

DAY 3   *"Only Luke is with me. Get Mark and bring him with you, because he is helpful to me in my ministry." (2 Timothy 4:11)*

REFLECT: _____

_____

_____

_____

_____

_____

_____

_____

_____

_____

DAY 4   *"I plead with Euodia and I plead with Syntyche to agree with each other in the Lord. Yes, and I ask you, loyal yokefellow, help these women who have contended at my side in the cause of the gospel, along with Clement and the rest of my fellow workers, whose names are in the book of life. Rejoice in the Lord always. I will say it again: Rejoice!" (Philippians 4:2–4)*

REFLECT: _____

_____

_____

_____

_____

_____

_____

_____

_____

_____

DAY 5   *"Therefore each of you must put off falsehood and speak truthfully to his neighbor, for we are all members of one body. 'In your anger do not sin': Do not let the sun go down while you are still angry, and do not give the devil a foothold." (Ephesians 4:25–27)*

REFLECT: _____

_____

_____

_____

_____

_____

_____

_____

_____

_____

_____

_____

DAY 6   Use the following space to write any thoughts God has put in your heart and mind about the things discussed during session five and/or during your Reflections time this week.

SUMMARY: _____

_____

_____

_____

_____

_____

_____

_____

_____

_____

_____

ELIJAH AND ELISHA — FRIENDS AND MENTORS

One of my most treasured relationships was one I was privileged to have with a couple twice my age. For a season I lived in their home and was allowed to experience their relationship firsthand. Even though they have both gone on to be with the Lord, theirs continues to be the most beautiful and successful marriage I have ever witnessed.

These two were so one with each other that when Horton had a massive, fatal heart attack, Edna had to have one of her own. Twenty minutes after finding him, she crumpled to the floor right in front of her doctor. She was rushed to the hospital where she exhibited all the symptoms of a heart attack, though later no evidence of heart damage could be clinically found. The doctor concluded that the emotional damage was so great her body had interpreted it as a physical heart attack in order to protect her from real injury.

Horton continues to be my best role model as a husband, if only through the pictures I still have of them both in my mind. He somehow managed to always keep Edna on her toes with loving surprises. I guarantee there has never been a happier or more fulfilled woman. Many a time I ask myself, "What would Horton do in this situation?" Whether I follow through is another story, but I am so much richer for this relationship.

 CONNECTING WITH GOD'S FAMILY   20 MIN.

Some of the most valued friendships we can cultivate are those that reach outside our "age group." Developing a close relationship with someone much older or much younger expands and enhances our lives. As we spend time with an older friend, we learn from them. We discover we are not alone in our life experiences. Moments invested in a younger life give us purpose for now — and hope for tomorrow. Elijah understood the time had come for him to consider succession planning, and he knew just who to ask for a suitable candidate. God directed him to Elisha, and a legendary friendship began.

1. Have you ever had, or do you now have, a close friend from another generation? What was/is that relationship like?

2. Take time in this final session to connect with your spiritual partner. What has God been showing you through these sessions about the nature of friendship and what he expects from you in relationship to others? Check in with each other about the progress you have made in your spiritual growth during this study. Make plans about whether you will continue in your mentoring relationship outside your Bible study group.

GROWING IN YOUR SPIRITUAL JOURNEY   40 MIN.

By now, Elijah had served God as a prophet to the continually wayward Israelites for many years. Would they ever get it right? As he grew older, Elijah sensed his assignment on earth was nearly over. Clearly, God needed someone younger to continue his work. He met Elisha, and the mentoring began.

Elijah's years of learning life's lessons straight from God made him the perfect mentor. Now Elijah asked his protégé, "What can I do for you while I am still here?" Boldly and without hesitation, Elisha asked—not for a token of Elijah's affection, not for a prayer of blessing—but for a double portion of his spirit!

According to Hebrew tradition, the firstborn son was entitled to a double portion of his father's inheritance. Elisha's request illustrates the close nature of his relationship with Elijah. He saw him as his spiritual father.

Knowing only God could give Elisha what he asked for, Elijah set up the means by which Elisha would know whether or not he would receive his request. God, who examines our hearts, gave Elisha what he had asked for. Elijah's ministry would be carried on.

Read 2 Kings 2:8–15:

> Elijah took his cloak, rolled it up and struck the water with it.
> The water divided to the right and to the left, and the two of
> them crossed over on dry ground. ⁹When they had crossed,
> Elijah said to Elisha, "Tell me, what can I do for you before I

am taken from you?" "Let me inherit a double portion of your spirit," Elisha replied. ¹⁰"You have asked a difficult thing," Elijah said, "yet if you see me when I am taken from you, it will be yours—otherwise not." ¹¹As they were walking along and talking together, suddenly a chariot of fire and horses of fire appeared and separated the two of them, and Elijah went up to heaven in a whirlwind. ¹²Elisha saw this and cried out, "My father! My father! The chariots and horsemen of Israel!" And Elisha saw him no more. Then he took hold of his own clothes and tore them apart. ¹³He picked up the cloak that had fallen from Elijah and went back and stood on the bank of the Jordan. ¹⁴Then he took the cloak that had fallen from him and struck the water with it. "Where now is the LORD, the God of Elijah?" he asked. When he struck the water, it divided to the right and to the left, and he crossed over. ¹⁵The company of the prophets from Jericho, who were watching, said, "The spirit of Elijah is resting on Elisha." And they went to meet him and bowed to the ground before him.

3. What do you think is significant about Elijah's cloak (verses 8, 13–14)?

4. Read 1 Kings 19:19. By what symbolic act had Elijah identified Elisha as his successor? How do you think Elisha recognized this calling?

5. It's hard sometimes to imagine we could ever be in the position of someone we respect and admire. How do you think you would respond if your pastor, your boss, your small group leader, or someone else in authority over you called tomorrow and asked you to take over his or her job?

6. Elijah's cloak is a symbol of his authority as a prophet. Is there an item in your life that reminds you of God's hand upon you? What is it? Share your story briefly with the group. Who could you pass it on to in a symbolic way?

7. Consider Elisha's request of Elijah in 2 Kings 2:9. What was he really asking? For help, see Deuteronomy 21:17.

8. Think for a moment about the incident described in verse 11. What does this say to us about the need to live every day as if it were our last, and to invest in others now while we still can?

9. Why do you think God granted Elisha's request?

FOR DEEPER STUDY

Consider a comparative study of Elijah and Elisha—two men whose lives are remarkably parallel:

- 2 Kings 2:8, 14
- 1 Kings 18:41–45; 2 Kings 3:9–20
- 1 Kings 17:10–16; 2 Kings 4:1–7
- 1 Kings 17:17–24; 2 Kings 4:18–35
- 1 Kings 17:9–16; 2 Kings 5:1–15
- 1 Kings 21:19–22; 2 Kings 8:7–10
- 2 Kings 1:9–12; 2:23–25

DEVELOPING YOUR GIFTS TO SERVE OTHERS 10 MIN.

Groups can be great places for mentoring relationships to develop. Perhaps someone in your group needs a double portion of what God has given you. What are you especially good at? Who can benefit from what you know about:

- The Bible?
- Raising kids?
- Having a healthy marriage?
- Serving Christ?
- Making wise investments?

Plan a time to get together with that person or group member to pass on what you know.

10. If your group still needs to make decisions about continuing to meet after this session, have that discussion now. Review your Small Group Agreement on pages 89–90, evaluate how well you met your goals, and discuss any changes you want to make as you move forward. Talk about what you will study, who will lead, and where and when you will meet.

SHARING YOUR LIFE MISSION EVERY DAY 10 MIN.

As prophets, both Elijah and Elisha recognized their messages were meaningless without someone to hear them. And they both understood, after years of frustration, that they might have to speak for years to what seemed like walls without ears before their message got through.

11. Who in your life have you been trying to reach but still is resisting God's message? Ask the group to pray with you for that person's heart to be softened and their ears opened to his call.

SURRENDERING YOUR LIFE FOR GOD'S PLEASURE 15–20 MIN.

God is so pleased when we let go of our own agendas and take up his mantle. As together you reflect in prayer on this study, share what God has asked you to give up in order to embrace a friendship for him.

12. If you have decided to share Communion together today, do so now. Instructions can be found on pages 98–99 of the appendix. This time of Communion will take some forethought and planning to make it special. Focus on your gratefulness for the connection you have with God and one another through the ministry of the Holy Spirit as you commemorate Christ's sacrifice for you.

    If you are not sharing Communion today, consider a time of praise instead. There is much to thank God for.

13. Consider planning a celebration soon in honor of the friendships God has given you in your group. If you plan to continue with this series on character, perhaps you could have your celebration before moving on to another topic.

14. Before you leave, remember to pray for any needs in the group and record your requests and praises on the Prayer and Praise Report on page 81.

STUDY NOTES

Elijah and Elisha. Elijah was the prophet who slayed the prophets of Baal and then in fear ran for his life from Queen Jezebel (see 1 Kings 18–19). As he sought refuge on Mount Horeb, God revealed himself in the sound of a gentle whisper. Elisha learned many lessons as Elijah's assistant and eventually became a great prophet like his predecessor.

Inherit a double portion of your spirit. This was more than a legal request to be the rightful heir of the prophet (Deuteronomy 21:17) but a sign of Elisha's need for the filling of the Spirit to continue in Elijah's footsteps. According to the *Zondervan NIV Bible Commentary,* "He wished, virtually, that Elijah's mighty prowess might continue to live through him."

Cloak. These were the clothes of Elijah, his mantle, that represented his authority. Now they were permanently on Elisha as a sign that the prophetic office had been passed on to him.

Briefly share your prayer requests with the large group, making notations below. Then gather in small groups of two to four to pray for each other.

Date: _____

PRAYER REQUESTS

_____

_____

_____

_____

_____

_____

_____

_____

_____

_____

PRAISE REPORT

_____

_____

_____

_____

_____

_____

_____

_____

REFLECTIONS

Each day read the daily verse(s) and give prayerful consideration to what you learn about God, his Spirit, and his place in your life. Then record your thoughts, insights, or prayer in the Reflect section. On day six record a summary of what you have learned over the entire week through this study.

DAY 1   *"Do not neglect your gift, which was given you through a prophetic message when the body of elders laid their hands on you. Be diligent in these matters; give yourself wholly to them, so that everyone may see your progress." (1 Timothy 4:14 – 15)*

REFLECT: _____

_____

_____

_____

_____

_____

_____

_____

DAY 2   *"May God himself, the God of peace, sanctify you through and through. May your whole spirit, soul and body be kept blameless at the coming of our Lord Jesus Christ. The one who calls you is faithful and he will do it." (1 Thessalonians 5:23 – 24)*

REFLECT: _____

_____

_____

_____

_____

_____

_____

DAY 3   *"Without good directon, people lose their way; the more wise counsel
you follow, the better your chances." (Proverbs 11:14 MSG)*

*"Arrogant know-it-alls stir up discord, but wise men and women
listen to each other's counsel." (Proverbs 13:10 MSG)*

REFLECT: _____

_____

_____

_____

_____

_____

_____

_____

_____

_____

_____

DAY 4   *"You then, my son, be strong in the grace that is in Christ Jesus. And
the things you have heard me say in the presence of many witnesses
entrust to reliable men who will also be qualified to teach others."
(2 Timothy 2:1–2)*

REFLECT: _____

_____

_____

_____

_____

_____

_____

_____

_____

_____

_____

DAY 5   *"The master said, 'Well done, my good and faithful servant. You have been faithful in handling this small amount, so now I will give you many more responsibilities. Let's celebrate together!'" (Matthew 25:23 NLT)*

REFLECT: _____

_____

_____

_____

_____

_____

_____

_____

_____

_____

_____

_____

DAY 6   Use the following space to write any thoughts God has put in your heart and mind about the things discussed during session six and/or during your Reflections time this week.

SUMMARY: _____

_____

_____

_____

_____

_____

_____

_____

_____

_____

_____

APPENDIX

FREQUENTLY ASKED QUESTIONS

WHAT DO WE DO ON THE FIRST NIGHT OF OUR GROUP?

Like all fun things in life—have a party! A "get to know you" coffee, dinner, or dessert is a great way to launch a new study. You may want to review the Small Group Agreement (pages 89–90) and share the names of a few friends you can invite to join you. But most importantly, have fun before your study time begins.

WHERE DO WE FIND NEW MEMBERS FOR OUR GROUP?

This can be troubling, especially for new groups that have only a few people or for existing groups that lose a few people along the way. We encourage you to pray with your group and then brainstorm a list of people from work, church, your neighborhood, your children's school, family, the gym, and so forth. Then have each group member invite several of the people on his or her list. Another good strategy is to ask church leaders to make an announcement or allow a bulletin insert.

No matter how you find members, it's vital that you stay on the lookout for new people to join your group. All groups tend to go through healthy attrition—the result of moves, releasing new leaders, ministry opportunities, and so forth—and if the group gets too small, it could be at risk of shutting down. If you and your group stay open, you'll be amazed at the people God sends your way. The next person just might become a friend for life. You never know!

HOW LONG WILL THIS GROUP MEET?

It's totally up to the group—once you come to the end of this six-week study. Most groups meet weekly for at least their first six weeks, but every other week can work as well. We strongly recommend that the group meet for the first six months on a weekly basis if at all possible. This allows for continuity, and if people miss a meeting they aren't gone for a whole month.

At the end of this study, each group member may decide if he or she wants to continue on for another six-week study. Some groups launch relationships for years to come, and others are stepping-stones into another group experience. Either way, enjoy the journey.

CAN WE DO THIS STUDY ON OUR OWN?

Absolutely! This may sound crazy but one of the best ways to do this study is not with a full house but with a few friends. You may choose to gather with one other couple who would enjoy going to the movies or having a quiet dinner and then walking through this study. Jesus will be with you even if there are only two of you (Matthew 18:20).

WHAT IF THIS GROUP IS NOT WORKING FOR US?

You're not alone! This could be the result of a personality conflict, life stage difference, geographical distance, level of spiritual maturity, or any number of things. Relax. Pray for God's direction, and at the end of this six-week study, decide whether to continue with this group or find another. You don't buy the first car you look at or marry the first person you date, and the same goes with a group. Don't bail out before the six weeks are up—God might have something to teach you. Also, don't run from conflict or prejudge people before you have given them a chance. God is still working in you too!

WHO IS THE LEADER?

Most groups have an official leader. But ideally, the group will mature and members will rotate the leadership of meetings. We have discovered that healthy groups rotate hosts/leaders and homes on a regular basis. This model ensures that all members grow, give their unique contribution, and develop their gifts. This study guide and the Holy Spirit can keep things on track even when you rotate leaders. Christ has promised to be in your midst as you gather. Ultimately, God is your leader each step of the way.

HOW DO WE HANDLE THE CHILD-CARE NEEDS IN OUR GROUP?

Very carefully. Seriously, this can be a sensitive issue. We suggest that you empower the group to openly brainstorm solutions. You may try one option that works for a while and then adjust over time. Our favorite approach is for adults to meet in the living room or dining room, and to share the cost of a babysitter (or two) who can be with the kids in a different part of the house. In this way, parents don't have to be away from their children all evening when their children are too young to be left at home. A second option is to use one home for the kids and a second home (close by or a phone call away) for the adults. A third idea is to rotate the responsibility of providing a lesson or care for the children either in the same home or in another home nearby. This can be an incredible blessing for kids. Finally, the most common idea is to decide that you need to have a night to invest in your spiritual lives individually or as a couple, and to make your own arrangements for child care. No matter what decision the group makes, the best approach is to dialogue openly about both the problem and the solution.

SMALL GROUP AGREEMENT

OUR PURPOSE

To transform our spiritual lives by cultivating our spiritual health in a healthy small group community. In addition, we: _____

_____

_____

_____

OUR VALUES

Group Attendance	To give priority to the group meeting. We will call or email if we will be late or absent. (Completing the Small Group Calendar on page 91 will minimize this issue.)
Safe Environment	To help create a safe place where people can be heard and feel loved. (Please, no quick answers, snap judgments, or simple fixes.)
Respect Differences	To be gentle and gracious to people with different spiritual maturity, personal opinions, temperaments, or imperfections. We are all works in progress.
Confidentiality	To keep anything that is shared strictly confidential and within the group, and to avoid sharing improper information about those outside the group.
Encouragement for Growth	To be not just takers but givers of life. We want to spiritually multiply our life by serving others with our God-given gifts.

Welcome for Newcomers	To keep an open chair and share Jesus' dream of finding a shepherd for every sheep.
Shared Ownership	To remember that every member is a minister and to ensure that each attender will share a small team role or responsibility over time.
Rotating Hosts/Leaders and Homes	To encourage different people to host the group in their homes, and to rotate the responsibility of facilitating each meeting. (See the Small Group Calendar on page 91.)

OUR EXPECTATIONS

- Refreshments/mealtimes _____
- Child care _____
- When we will meet (day of week) _____
- Where we will meet (place) _____
- We will begin at (time) _____ and end at _____
- We will do our best to have some or all of us attend a worship service together. Our primary worship service time will be _____
- Date of this agreement _____
- Date we will review this agreement again _____
- Who (other than the leader) will review this agreement at the end of this study _____

SMALL GROUP CALENDAR

Planning and calendaring can help ensure the greatest participation at every meeting. At the end of each meeting, review this calendar. Be sure to include a regular rotation of host homes and leaders, and don't forget birthdays, socials, church events, holidays, and mission/ministry projects.

Date	Lesson	Host Home	Dessert/Meal	Leader
Monday, January 15	1	Steve/Laura's	Joe	Bill

PERSONAL HEALTH PLAN

This worksheet could become your single most important feature in this study. On it you can record your personal priorities before the Father. It will help you live a healthy spiritual life, balancing all five of God's purposes.

PURPOSE	PLAN
CONNECT	WHO are you connecting with spiritually?
GROW	WHAT is your next step for growth?
DEVELOP	WHERE are you serving?
SHARE	WHEN are you shepherding another in Christ?
SURRENDER	HOW are you surrendering your heart?

DATE	MY PROGRESS	PARTNER'S PROGRESS

SAMPLE
PERSONAL HEALTH PLAN

This worksheet could become your single most important feature in this study. On it you can record your personal priorities before the Father. It will help you live a healthy spiritual life, balancing all five of God's purposes.

PURPOSE	PLAN
CONNECT	WHO are you connecting with spiritually? *Bill and I will meet weekly by email or phone*
GROW	WHAT is your next step for growth? *Regular devotions or journaling my prayers 2x/week*
DEVELOP	WHERE are you serving? *Serving in Children's Ministry* *Go through GIFTS Class*
SHARE	WHEN are you shepherding another in Christ? *Shepherding Bill at lunch or hosting a starter group in the fall*
SURRENDER	HOW are you surrendering your heart? *Help with our teenager* *New job situation*

DATE	MY PROGRESS	PARTNER'S PROGRESS
3/5	Talked during our group	Figured out our goals together
3/12	Missed our time together	Missed our time together
3/26	Met for coffee and review of my goals	Met for coffee
4/10	Emailed prayer requests	Bill sent me his prayer requests
3/5	Great start on personal journaling	Read Mark 1 – 6 in one sitting!
3/12	Traveled and not doing well this week	Journaled about Christ as Healer
3/26	Back on track	Busy and distracted; asked for prayer
3/1	Need to call Children's Pastor	
3/26	Group did a serving project together	Agreed to lead group worship
3/30	Regularly rotating leadership	Led group worship — great job!
3/5	Called Jim to see if he's open to joining our group	Wanted to invite somebody, but didn't
3/12	Preparing to start a group in fall	
3/30	Group prayed for me	Told friend something he's learning about Christ
3/5	Overwhelmed but encouraged	Scared to lead worship
3/15	Felt heard and more settled	Issue with wife
3/30	Read book on teens	Glad he took on his fear

PERSONAL HEALTH ASSESSMENT

	JUST BEGINNING	GETTING GOING	WELL DEVELOPED

CONNECTING WITH GOD AND OTHERS

I am deepening my understanding of and friendship
with God in community with others.　　1　2　3　4　5

I am growing in my ability both to share and to
show my love to others.　　1　2　3　4　5

I am willing to share my real needs for prayer and
support from others.　　1　2　3　4　5

I am resolving conflict constructively and am
willing to forgive others.　　1　2　3　4　5

CONNECTING TOTAL _____

GROWING IN YOUR SPIRITUAL JOURNEY

I have a growing relationship with God through regular
time in the Bible and in prayer (spiritual habits).　　1　2　3　4　5

I am experiencing more of the characteristics of
Jesus Christ (love, patience, gentleness, courage,
self-control, and so forth) in my life.　　1　2　3　4　5

I am avoiding addictive behaviors (food, television,
busyness, and the like) to meet my needs.　　1　2　3　4　5

I am spending time with a Christian friend (spiritual partner)
who celebrates and challenges my spiritual growth.　　1　2　3　4　5

GROWING TOTAL _____

SERVING WITH YOUR GOD-GIVEN DESIGN

I have discovered and am further developing my
unique God-given design.　　1　2　3　4　5

I am regularly praying for God to show me
opportunities to serve him and others.　　1　2　3　4　5

I am serving in a regular (once a month or more)
ministry in the church or community.　　1　2　3　4　5

I am a team player in my small group by sharing
some group role or responsibility.　　1　2　3　4　5

SERVING TOTAL _____

SHARING GOD'S LOVE IN EVERYDAY LIFE

I am cultivating relationships with non-Christians and praying
for God to give me natural opportunities to share his love.   1   2   3   4   5

I am praying and learning about where God can use me
and my group cross-culturally for missions.   1   2   3   4   5

I am investing my time in another person or group who
needs to know Christ.   1   2   3   4   5

I am regularly inviting unchurched or unconnected
friends to my church or small group.   1   2   3   4   5

SHARING TOTAL _____

SURRENDERING YOUR LIFE TO GOD

I am experiencing more of the presence and
power of God in my everyday life.   1   2   3   4   5

I am faithfully attending services and my
small group to worship God.   1   2   3   4   5

I am seeking to please God by surrendering every
area of my life (health, decisions, finances,
relationships, future, and the like) to him.   1   2   3   4   5

I am accepting the things I cannot change and
becoming increasingly grateful for the life I've been given.   1   2   3   4   5

SURRENDERING TOTAL _____

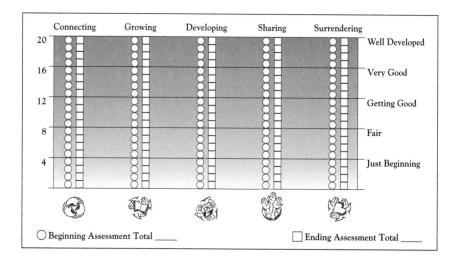

SERVING COMMUNION

The Lord Jesus, on the night he was betrayed, took bread, and when he had given thanks, he broke it and said, "This is my body, which is for you; do this in remembrance of me." In the same way, after supper he took the cup, saying, "This cup is the new covenant in my blood; do this, whenever you drink, in remembrance of me." For whenever you eat this bread and drink this cup, you proclaim the Lord's death until he comes. (1 Corinthians 11:23–26)

SEVERAL PRACTICAL TIPS IN SERVING COMMUNION

1. Be sensitive to timing in your meeting.
2. Break up pieces of cracker or soft bread on a small plate or tray. *Don't* use large servings of bread or grape juice. We ask that you only use grape juice, not wine, so you will not cause a group member to struggle.
3. Prepare all of the elements beforehand and bring these into the room when you are ready.

STEPS IN SERVING COMMUNION

1. Open by sharing about God's love, forgiveness, grace, mercy, commitment, tenderheartedness, or faithfulness, out of your own personal journey (connect with the stories of those in the room).
2. Read the passage: "The Lord Jesus, on the night he was betrayed, took bread, and when he had given thanks, he broke it and said, 'This is my body, which is for you; do this in remembrance of me.'"
3. Pray and pass the bread around the circle (could be time for quiet reflection, singing a simple praise song, or listening to a worship CD).
4. When everyone has been served, remind them that this represents Jesus' broken body on their behalf. Simply state, "Jesus said, 'Do this

in remembrance of me.' Let us eat together," and eat the bread as a group.

5. Then read the rest of the passage: "In the same way, after supper he took the cup, saying, 'This cup is the new covenant in my blood; do this, whenever you drink it, in remembrance of me.'"

6. Pray and serve the cups, either by passing a small tray, serving them individually, or having members pick up a cup from the table.

7. When everyone has been served, remind them the juice represents Christ's blood shed for them, then simply state, "Take and drink in remembrance of him. Let us drink together."

8. Finish by singing a simple song, listening to a praise song, or having a time of prayer in thanks to God.

Communion passages: Matthew 26:26–29; Mark 14:22–25; Luke 22:14–20; 1 Corinthians 10:16–21; 11:17–34

LEADING
FOR THE FIRST TIME

- **Sweaty palms are a healthy sign.** The Bible says God is gracious to the humble. Remember who is in control; the time to worry is when you're not worried. Those who are soft in heart (and sweaty palmed) are those whom God is sure to speak through.
- **Seek support.** Ask your leader, coleader, or close friend to pray for you and prepare with you before the session. Walking through the study will help you anticipate potentially difficult questions and discussion topics.
- **Bring your uniqueness to the study.** Lean into who you are and how God wants you to uniquely lead the study.
- **Prepare. Prepare. Prepare.** Read the Introduction and Leader's Notes for the session you are leading. Consider writing in a journal or fasting for a day to prepare yourself for what God wants to do.
- **Don't wait until the last minute to prepare.**
- **Ask for feedback so you can grow.** Perhaps in an email or on cards handed out at the study, have everyone write down three things you did well and one thing you could improve on. Don't get defensive, but show an openness to learn and grow.
- **Prayerfully consider launching a new group.** This doesn't need to happen overnight, but God's heart is for this to happen over time. Not all Christians are called to be leaders or teachers, but we are all called to be "shepherds" of a few someday.
- **Share with your group what God is doing in your heart.** God is searching for those whose hearts are fully his. Share your trials and victories. We promise that people will relate.

INTRODUCTION

Congratulations! You have responded to the call to help shepherd Jesus' flock. There are few other tasks in the family of God that surpass the contribution you will be making. As you prepare to lead this small group, there are a few thoughts to keep in mind:

Review the "Read Me First" on pages 9–11 so you'll understand the purpose of each section in the study. If this is your first time leading a small group, turn to Leading for the First Time section on page 100 of the appendix for suggestions.

Remember that you are not alone. God knows everything about you, and he knew that you would be leading this group. God promises, "Never will I leave you; never will I forsake you" (Hebrews 13:5b).

Your role as leader. Create a safe, warm environment for your group. As a leader, your most important job is to create an atmosphere where people are willing to talk honestly about what the topics discussed in this study have to do with them. Be available before people arrive so you can greet them at the door. People are naturally nervous at a new group, so a hug or handshake can help put them at ease.

Prepare for each meeting ahead of time. Review the Leader's Notes and write down your responses to each study question. Pay special attention to exercises that ask group members to do something other than engage in discussion. These exercises will help your group live what the Bible teaches, not just talk about it. Be sure you understand how an exercise works, and bring any necessary supplies (such a paper or pens) to your meeting.

Pray for your group members by name. Before you begin each session, go around the room in your mind and pray for each member by name. You may want to review the prayer list at least once a week. Ask God to use your time together to touch the heart of every person uniquely. Expect God to lead you to those he wants you to encourage or challenge in a special way.

Discuss expectations. Ask everyone to tell what he or she hopes to get out of this study. You might want to review the Small Group Agreement (see pages 89–90) and talk about each person's expectations and priorities. You could discuss whether you want to do the For Deeper Study for homework before each meeting. Review the Small Group Calendar on page 91 and talk about who else is willing to open their home to host or facilitate a meeting.

Don't try to go it alone. Pray for God to help you, and enlist help from the members of your group. You will find your experience to be richer and more rewarding if you enable group members to help—and you'll be able to help group members discover their individual gifts for serving or even leading the group.

Plan a kick-off meeting. We recommend that you plan a kick-off meeting where you will pray, hand out study guides, spend some time getting to know each other, and discuss each person's expectations for the group. A meeting like this is a great way to start a group or step up people's commitments.

A simple meal, potluck, or even good desserts make a kick-off meeting more fun. After dessert, have everyone respond to an icebreaker question, such as, "How did you hear of our church, and what's one thing you love about it?" Or, "Tell us three things about your life growing up that most people here don't know."

If you aren't able to hold a "get to know you" meeting before you launch into session one, consider starting the first meeting half an hour early to give people time to socialize without shortchanging your time in the study. For example, you can have social time from 7:00 to 7:30, and by 7:40 you'll gather the group with a prayer. Even if only a few people are seated in the living room by 7:40, ask them to join you in praying for those who are coming and for God to be present among you as you meet. Others will notice you praying and will come and sit down. You may want to softly play music from a LIFE TOGETHER Worship CD or other worship CD as people arrive and then turn up the volume when you are ready to begin. This first night will set the tone for the whole six weeks.

You may ask a few people to come early to help set up, pray, and introduce newcomers to others. Even if everyone is new, they don't know that yet and may be shy when they arrive. You might give people roles like setting up name tags or handing out drinks. This could be a great way to spot a coleader.

Subgrouping. If your group has more than seven people, break into discussion groups of two to four people for the Growing and Surrendering sections each week. People will connect more with the study and each other when they have more opportunity to participate. Smaller discussion circles encourage quieter people to talk more and tend to minimize the effects of more vocal or dominant members. Also, people who are unaccustomed to praying aloud will feel more comfortable praying within a smaller group of people. Consider sharing prayer requests in the larger group and then break into smaller groups to pray for each other. People are more willing to pray in small circles if they know that the whole group will hear all the prayer requests.

Memorizing Scripture. Although we have not provided specific verses for the group to memorize, this is something you can encourage the group to do each week. One benefit of memorizing God's Word is noted by the psalmist in Psalm 119:11: "I have hidden your word in my heart that I might not sin against you."

Anyone who has memorized Scripture can confirm the amazing spiritual benefits that result from this practice. Don't miss out on the opportunity to encourage your group to grow in the knowledge of God's Word through Scripture memorization.

Reflections. We've provided opportunity for a personal time with God using the Reflections at the end of each session. Don't press seekers to do this, but just remind the group that every believer should have a plan for personal time with God.

Invite new people. Finally, cast the vision, as Jesus did, to be inclusive not exclusive. Ask everyone to prayerfully think of people who would enjoy or benefit from a group like this. The beginning of a new study is a great time to welcome a few people into your circle. Have each person share a name or two and either make phone calls the coming week or handwrite invitations or postcards that very night. This will make it fun and also make it happen. Don't worry about ending up with too many people — you can always have one discussion circle in the living room and another in the dining room.

SESSION 1: DAVID AND JONATHAN — FRIENDS FOR LIFE

As a leader, your most important job is to create an atmosphere where people are willing to talk honestly about what the topics discussed in this study have to do with them. If your group is new and you aren't able to hold a kick-off meeting before you launch into session one, consider starting your first meeting half an hour early to give people time to socialize without short-changing your time in the study. For example, you can have social time from 7:00 to 7:30, and by 7:40 you'll gather the group with a prayer. Even if only a few people are seated in the living room by 7:40, ask them to join you in prayer for those who are coming and for God to be present among you as you meet. Others will notice you praying and will come and sit down. You may want to softly play music from a LIFE TOGETHER Worship DVD/CD (you can find them at www.lifetogether.com) or other worship CD as people arrive, and turn up the volume when you are ready to begin. This first night will set the tone for the whole six weeks.

You may want to ask a few people to come early to help set up, pray, and introduce newcomers to others. Even if everyone is new, they don't know that yet and may be shy when they arrive. You might give people roles like setting up name tags or handing out drinks. This could be a great way to spot a coleader.

CONNECTING. Question 1. We've designed this study for both new and established groups. New groups need to invest more time in building relationships with each other, while established groups often want to dig deeper into Bible study and application. Begin your group time with this icebreaker question to get people relaxed and focused on the session topic. You should be the first to answer this question while others are thinking about how to respond. Be sure to give everyone a chance to respond, because it's a chance for the group to get to know each other. It's not necessary to go around the circle in order. Just ask for volunteers to respond.

Introduction to the Series. Take a moment after question 1 to orient the group to one principle that undergirds this series: A healthy small group balances the purposes of the church. Most small groups emphasize Bible study, fellowship, and prayer. But God has called us to reach out to others as well.

He wants us to *do* what Jesus teaches, not just *learn* about it. You may spend less time in this series studying the Bible than some group members are used to. That's because you'll spend more time *doing* things the Bible says believers should do.

However, those who like more Bible study can find plenty of it in this series. For Deeper Study provides additional passages you can study on the topic of each session. If your group likes to do deeper Bible study, consider having members answer next week's Growing section questions ahead of time as homework. They can even study next week's For Deeper Study passages for homework too. Then, during the Growing portion of your meeting, you can share the high points of what you've learned.

If the five biblical purposes are new to your group, be sure to review them together on pages 9–11 of the Read Me First section.

Question 2. A Small Group Agreement helps you clarify your group's priorities and cast new vision for what the group can be. Members can imagine what your group could be like if they lived these values. So turn to pages 89–90 and choose one or two values that you want to emphasize in this study.

We've suggested reviewing the Frequently Asked Questions to gain an understanding of how the group should function and answer any questions that may come up. Also don't forget to give opportunity to get an up-to-date Small Group Roster started during this time (see pages 117–118).

Question 3. If you choose "Rotating Leaders" as a key value, you don't need to invest a lot of time in it now. In session two you'll have a chance to plan who will host and lead each meeting.

GROWING. Each Growing section begins with an opening story and a passage of Scripture. Have someone read the opening story and someone else read the Bible passage aloud. It's a good idea to ask someone ahead of time, because not everyone is comfortable reading aloud in public. When the passage has been read, ask the questions that follow. It is not necessary that everyone answer every question in the Bible study. In fact, a group can become boring if you simply go around the circle and give answers. Your goal is to create a discussion—which means that perhaps only a few people respond to each question and an engaging dialogue gets going. It's even fine to skip some questions in order to spend more time on questions you believe are most important.

Remember to use the Study Notes as you go through this section to add depth and understanding to your study.

Questions 4–11. For this section you might want to have several different Bible translations available for comparing the wording of 1 Samuel 18. The story of David and Jonathan's friendship is one of the most well-known in Scripture. Their friendship was built on a covenant entered into before God. God was central to the relationship and their commitment to one another was binding before him. Read the Study Notes and any commentary notes in your study Bible for help understanding the covenant commitment they made to one another. You will find an understanding of God's view of covenant to be helpful as you address the questions in this section.

DEVELOPING. Question 12. Jonathan encouraged David in the Lord during a stressful time of his life. As believers, we can also be a source of encouragement to others in difficult times. Plan your discussion time so you have an opportunity to address practical ways to offer meaningful encouragement not only to those within the group but to other Christ-followers.

Question 13. Here is your opportunity to encourage your group to embrace Scripture reading and time with God by using the Reflections throughout the week. Remind them of how regular time with God and his Word will reap the reward of spiritual growth for those willing to give themselves to it. Maybe you or someone else in the group can share a personal story of the impact this important habit has made on you.

Question 14. For those who haven't done a LIFE TOGETHER study before, spiritual partners will be a new idea. This addresses the practice of having an accountability partner, someone who will commit to pray and hold you accountable for spiritual goals and progress. This may be the single most important habit your group members can take away from this study. Encourage everyone to partner with one other person, two at the most. In this session we encourage you to become familiar with and begin to use the Personal Health Plan to challenge and track your spiritual goals and progress as well as your partner's. There is one Personal Health Plan in the appendix of this book so be sure to have a few extra copies on hand at your first meeting for groups of three spiritual partners.

SHARING. Question 15. God calls all believers to share the good news about Jesus with those who don't know him. Challenge the group to make the most of this opportunity to reach out to a seeker or someone who isn't even sure that God exists. Have them write at least one person's name in the space provided. Encourage group members to pray for an opportunity to get to know them more, invite them to the group, or share a part of their own story with them. Encourage your group to do their part and trust God to touch the hearts of those they have listed.

SURRENDERING. Question 17. One of the most important aspects of every small group meeting is the prayer support we offer to one another. The Surrendering section gives you the opportunity to share needs and know that the group will be faithful to pray. As leader, you want to be sure to allow adequate time for this key component of small group life.

Never pressure a person to pray aloud. That's a sure way to scare someone away from your group. Instead of praying in a circle (which makes it obvious when someone stays silent), allow open time when anyone can pray who wishes to do so. Have someone write down everyone's prayer requests on the Prayer and Praise Report. If your time is short, consider having people share requests and pray only with their spiritual partners or in circles of two to four.

SESSION 2: RUTH AND NAOMI — CONNECTED THROUGH LOSS

As you begin, welcome any new people and praise the ones who brought them. Renew the vision to welcome people for one more week and model this if you can. Then have everyone sit back, relax, close their eyes, and listen to one of the songs on a LIFE TOGETHER Worship CD, or other worship CD. You may want to sing the second time through as a group, or simply take a few moments of silence to focus on God and transition from the distractions of your day.

CONNECT. Questions 1–2. Checking in with your spiritual partners (question 1) will be an option in all sessions from now on. You'll need to watch the clock and keep these conversations to ten minutes. If partners want more time together (as is ideal), they can connect before, after, or outside meetings. Give them a two-minute notice and hold to it if you ever want to get them back in the circle! If some group members are absent or newcomers have joined you, you may need to connect people with new or temporary partners.

If you prefer (and especially if there are many newcomers), you can choose to use the lighter icebreaker question for the whole group. We encourage you, though, to let partners check in during group time at least every other week so that those relationships grow solid. Please don't miss this opportunity to take your people deeper. Remember that the goal here is "transforming lives through community," and one-on-one time has an enormous return on time spent. In a week or two, you might want to ask the group how their partnerships are going. This will encourage those who are struggling to connect or accomplish their goals.

If newcomers have joined you, take a few minutes before the Growing section to let all members introduce themselves. If you use the icebreaker question, you could even let each member share one thing he or she has liked about the group so far, and let the newcomers tell who invited them. The first visit to a new group is scary, so be sure to minimize the inside jokes. Introduce newcomers to some highly relational people when they arrive and partner them with great spiritual partners to welcome them at their first meeting.

We highly recommend that, as leader, you read the Study Notes ahead of time and draw the group's attention to anything there that will help them understand the Bible passage and how it applies to their lives.

DEVELOPING. Question 12. Here we talk about rotating host homes. This practice of rotating homes and leaders will help you to spot potential leaders and those who can fill in for you when you are unavailable for some reason. This is an important practice if you are going to help your group develop their gifts and build strong leaders within your group.

SHARING. Question 13. We ask you to go back to session one, question 15 to see if everyone has met their goals of influencing someone for Christ. Be sure to take time for this follow-up exercise. If people have not followed through yet, encourage them to make a plan and take the first step within the next twenty-four hours. Maybe they need to create an opportunity to get to know this person better, maybe begin to share their own experience as a Christian, or maybe be willing to address any questions the other person has. Whatever the need, encourage the group to be available.

Question 14. The Circles of Life diagram represents one of the values of the Small Group Agreement: "Welcome for Newcomers." Some groups fear that newcomers will interrupt the intimacy that members have built over time. However, groups generally gain strength with the infusion of new blood. It's like a river of living water flowing into a stagnant pond.

Some groups remain permanently open, while others open periodically, such as at the beginning and end of a study. Love grows by giving itself away. If your circle becomes too large for easy, face-to-face conversations, you can simply form a second discussion circle in another room in your home.

As leader, you should do this exercise yourself in advance and be ready to share the names of the people you're going to invite or connect with. Your modeling is the number-one example that people will follow. Give everyone a few moments to write down names before each person shares. You might pray for a few of these names on the spot and/or later in the session. Encourage people not to be afraid to ask someone. Almost no one is annoyed to be invited to something! Most people are honored to be asked, even if they can't make it. You may want to hand out invitations and fill them out in the group.

SURRENDERING. Question 15. Take time before you meet with the group to understand this exercise in the Surrendering section. This can be a group activity for turning a Scripture into a group prayer or you can have the group write out their own personal prayer.

Question 16. We've provided opportunity for a personal time with God throughout the week using the Reflections at the end of each session. Don't press seekers to do this, but every believer should have a plan for personal time with God.

SESSION 3: JESUS AND PETER— FAITHFUL FRIENDS

In order to maximize your time together and honor the diversity of personality types, do your best to begin and end your meeting on time. Remember, if you wait for people to arrive before starting, you are training them to know they aren't really late. If your group meets on weeknights when people need to get up early the next morning, it is unfair to begin and end later than you agreed upon. You may even want to adjust your starting or stopping time if it seems necessary. Don't hesitate to open in prayer even before everyone is seated. This isn't disrespectful of those who are still gathering—it respects those who are ready to begin, and the others won't be offended. An opening prayer can be as simple as, "Welcome, Lord! Help us! Now let's start."

If you've had trouble getting through all of the Bible study questions, consider breaking into smaller circles of four or five people for the Bible study (Growing) portion of your meeting. Everyone will get more "airtime," and the people who tend to dominate the discussion will be balanced out. A circle of four doesn't need an experienced leader, and it's a great way to identify and train a coleader. Also remember that if people are silent before they answer a question, it's because they're thinking!

GROWING. For the Growing section, be sure to familiarize yourself with the Study Notes so you can help the group understand how Peter understood Jesus' questions. This understanding can bring clarity as you discuss the questions in this section.

DEVELOPING. Question 10. This question provides your group the opportunity to consider who each group member can influence and strengthen in their spiritual journey. Encourage the group to recognize that you don't have to be a spiritual giant before you can be an encouragement to someone. We just need to be willing to invest in someone's life.

SHARING. Question 11. We all need someone to invest in our own lives, so we have also included a challenge to find someone to shepherd us. If someone believes there is no one who can take them further in their spiritual life, be sure to pray for the Lord to provide insight and clarity about the situation.

Question 12. Return to the Circles of Life diagram on page 33 to see if the people needing invitations to join the group have been contacted yet. If not, encourage members to make sure they call within the next twenty-four hours.

SURRENDERING. Question 16. Be sure to save time to pray for each other. In this session we have encouraged you to break into small groups of two or three for prayer.

There are bound to be people in your group who long for healing, whether physical or emotional, and this will come out during prayer request time. Some churches emphasize prayer for healing—if yours does, follow your church's practice in the way you approach this. Other churches prefer to avoid a charismatic flavor in their small groups—if yours has that concern, pray for one another in whatever way seems comfortable. If you're concerned that some members might confuse or try to "fix" others through prayer, pray as a whole group and monitor how people pray. But don't be overly concerned: the very worst that will happen is that someone will pray in a way that distresses someone else, and if that happens you can simply talk to each person privately before your next meeting. As leader, you set the example of how people will pray for each other in your group, and most members will follow your lead.

SESSION 4: PHILIP AND THE EUNICH — INTERRUPTED FOR GOD

The Bible is clear that every Christian is meant to be a servant of Christ. We strongly recommend you challenge your members to take whatever step that they sense God is calling them to and that will challenge them. You will need to model here. Don't miss the need people have to grow through sharing responsibilities to host the group.

CONNECTING. Question 1. This question is intended to get group members thinking about opportunities that God presents to us every day and what we choose to do with them. Encourage group members to prayerfully consider their own responses in these situations.

Question 2. As you encourage your group members to check in with their spiritual partners this week, you might want to ask the group to share how their partnerships are going. This will encourage those who are struggling to connect or accomplish their goals.

DEVELOPING. Question 9. Service should always be an expression of love. Among the people of God, no one should be forced to serve or be manipulated into serving. Those who serve because they fear those they serve, or because of guilt or manipulation, need the church's support in addressing those situations. The most loving thing the community can do for those who demand service, or who manipulate others, is to confront them about this behavior. Jesus was fearless and not subject to manipulation, so he could serve out of love. When you lead your group through this exercise of making a list of their God-given abilities, urge them to focus on those abilities that express love for his sake.

Question 10. This question is key. People need to go beyond theorizing about service to actually doing it. Try to come to this question prepared to get the discussion started with your own personal examples and ideas. Also, ask your pastor if there are any needs in the congregation that your group could fill: an elderly person who could use a Saturday morning yard cleanup, or someone just out of the hospital who is not yet able to clean house.

Question 11. In this session we want you to be thinking about this group continuing to meet for another study. Begin thinking about whether your group will continue to meet and what you can study next.

SHARING. Questions 12 – 13. Select among these questions to the degree you have time. Groups doing deeper Bible study will want to spend more time with these questions. Others may want to choose one of the two questions to discuss.

SURRENDERING. Question 14. Have someone read the first Bible passage aloud. It's a good idea to ask someone ahead of time, because not everyone is comfortable reading aloud in public. When the passage has been read, ask the group to discuss Philip's response to the angel's instructions. Then have someone read the second Bible passage aloud. Ask group members to evaluate their life as it relates to their readiness to act on behalf of others. Have group members share prayer requests about this during question 15.

Question 15. Have the group share their prayer requests and be sure to use the Prayer and Praise Report to record the requests. Having the prayer requests written down will prompt you to pray for each member, as well as remind you of God's faithfulness, as your groups sees their prayers answered. After requests have been recorded, spend some time praying as a group. Encourage group members to continue to pray for the group between meetings.

SESSION 5: PAUL AND BARNABAS—CONFLICT MANAGEMENT

Remember, in order to maximize your time together and honor your group, do your best to begin and end your meeting on time. Announce the opening prayer, even before everyone is seated, to indicate to the group that you are ready to begin.

CONNECTING. Question 1. Start out by having your members check in with their spiritual partner, and assess how they are doing with their Health Plans and the goals they have set for themselves.

DEVELOPING. Questions 9–11. Select among these questions to the degree you have time. We encourage an outward focus for your group because groups that become too inwardly focused tend to become unhealthy over time. People naturally gravitate to feeding themselves through Bible study, prayer, and social time, so it's usually up to the leader to push them to consider how this inward nourishment can overflow into outward concern for others. Never forget: Jesus came to seek and save the lost and to find a shepherd for every sheep.

You may want to affirm someone who is or has been a servant in your group—maybe behind the scenes—and then ask the group to do the same for others.

SHARING. Question 12. Encourage group members to think about living a life that demonstrates what a Christ-filled life looks like.

SURRENDERING. Question 15. Celebrating Communion can be a great way to end your study. Consider whether this is appropriate for your group. If so, make the necessary plans now.

SESSION 6: ELIJAH AND ELISHA — FRIENDS AND MENTORS

You made it! This is the last session of this study! It's time to celebrate where you've been and look forward to what's next for each of you and your group. If this is your first time leading the study, congratulations. Your goal for this meeting is to finish strong. It's also a time to think about God's final, ultimate purpose for you: surrendering your whole lives to him in worship, to give him pleasure.

CONNECTING. Question 2. Be sure to have spiritual partners check in with each other at this last meeting. Encourage them to review their Health Plans together to assess where they have grown and where they would still like to grow.

DEVELOPING. Question 10. Spend some time preparing your group to move forward. If your group is staying together, hopefully you've chosen your next study; be sure to take the study guides to the meeting. Suggest that the group take another look at your Small Group Agreement to see if you want to change anything for the next study. Are all the values working for you, or is there some way your group could be improved by changing your expectations or living up to one of these values better than you have been? You can make people feel safe talking about things they want to improve by first asking them what they've liked about the group. Set a positive tone. Then make sure people get to disagree respectfully, that everyone understands that they're speaking in confidence and won't be talked about outside the group, and that the goal of any changes will be the spiritual health of everyone.

SHARING. Question 11. This question is to provoke thought about obediently speaking out for God. He will do his part when we are obedient. Include any prayer requests expressed at this time in your prayer time at the end of the study.

SURRENDERING. Question 12. If you have decided to share Communion as a group at this final meeting, be sure to coordinate this ahead of time. Instructions can be found in the appendix on pages 98–99. Communion will probably take ten minutes if you have everything prepared. It's a tremendously moving experience in a small group.

If you will not be sharing Communion as a group, you might plan a time of praising God together instead. Take turns praying, using phrases like "Thank you, Lord, for ..." or "Lord, I praise you for ..." to begin.

Questions 13 – 14. Whether your group is ending or continuing, it's important to celebrate where you have come together. Thank everyone for what they've contributed to the group. You might even give some thought ahead of time to something unique each person has contributed. Share your prayer requests and pray for each other before you close your meeting.

SMALL GROUP ROSTER

Name	Address	Phone	Email Address	Team or Role	Church Ministry
Bill Jones	7 Alralar Street L.F. 92665	766-2255	bjones@aol.com	Socials	children's ministry

(Pass your book around your group at your first meeting to get everyone's name and contact information.)

Name	Address	Phone	Email Address	Team or Role	Church Ministry

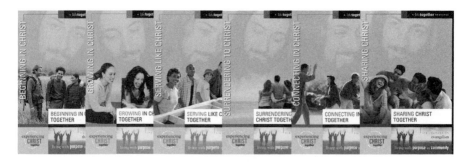

Experiencing Christ Together:

Living with Purpose in Community

Brett & Dee Eastman; Todd & Denise Wendorff; Karen Lee-Thorp

Experiencing Christ Together: Living with Purpose in Community is a series of six, six-week study guides that offers small groups a chance to explore Jesus' teaching on the five biblical purposes of the church. By closely examining Christ's life and teaching in the Gospels, the series helps group members walk in the steps of Christ's early followers. Jesus lived every moment following God's purposes for his life, and Experiencing Christ Together helps groups learn how they can do this too. The first book lays the foundation: who Christ is and what he has done for us. Each of the other five books in the series looks at how Jesus trained his followers to live one of the five biblical purposes (fellowship, discipleship, service, evangelism, and worship).

	Softcovers	DVD
Beginning in Christ Together	ISBN: 0-310-24986-4	ISBN: 0-310-26187-2
Connecting in Christ Together	ISBN: 0-310-24981-3	ISBN: 0-310-26189-9
Growing in Christ Together	ISBN: 0-310-24985-6	ISBN: 0-310-26192-9
Serving Like Christ Together	ISBN: 0-310-24984-8	ISBN: 0-310-26194-5
Sharing Christ Together	ISBN: 0-310-24983-X	ISBN: 0-310-26196-1
Surrendering to Christ Together	ISBN: 0-310-24982-1	ISBN: 0-310-26198-8

Pick up a copy today at your favorite bookstore!

Doing Life Together series

Brett & Dee Eastman; Todd & Denise Wendorff; Karen Lee-Thorp

Based on the five biblical purposes that form the bedrock of Saddleback Church, Doing Life Together will help your group discover what God created you for and how you can turn this dream into an everyday reality. Experience the transformation firsthand as you begin Connecting, Growing, Developing, Sharing, and Surrendering your life together for him.

"Doing Life Together is a groundbreaking study . . . [It's] the first small group curriculum built completely on the purpose-driven paradigm . . . The greatest reason I'm excited about [it] is that I've seen the dramatic changes it produces in the lives of those who study it."

—From the foreword by Rick Warren

Small Group Ministry Consultation

Building a healthy, vibrant, and growing small group ministry is challenging. That's why Brett Eastman and a team of certified coaches are offering small group ministry consultation. Join pastors and church leaders from around the country to discover new ways to launch and lead a healthy Purpose-Driven small group ministry in your church. To find out more information please call 1-800-467-1977.

	Softcover	
Beginning Life Together	ISBN: 0-310-24672-5	ISBN: 0-310-25004-8
Connecting with God's Family	ISBN: 0-310-24673-3	ISBN: 0-310-25005-6
Growing to Be Like Christ	ISBN: 0-310-24674-1	ISBN: 0-310-25006-4
Developing Your SHAPE to Serve Others	ISBN: 0-310-24675-X	ISBN: 0-310-25007-2
Sharing Your Life Mission Every Day	ISBN: 0-310-24676-8	ISBN: 0-310-25008-0
Surrendering Your Life for God's Pleasure	ISBN: 0-310-24677-6	ISBN: 0-310-25009-9
Curriculum Kit	ISBN: 0-310-25002-1	

Life Together Student Edition

Brett Eastman & Doug Fields

The Life Together series is the beginning of a relational journey, from being a member of a group to being a vital part of an unbelievable spiritual community. These books will help you think, talk, dig deep, care, heal, share . . . and have the time of your life! Life . . . together!

The Life Together Student Edition DVD Curriculum combines DVD teaching from well-known youth Bible teachers, as well as leadership training, with the Life Together Student Edition Small Group Series to give a new way to do small group study and ministry with basic training on how to live healthy and balanced lives-purpose driven lives.

Pick up a copy today at your favorite bookstore!

We want to hear from you. Please send your comments about this book to us in care of zreview@zondervan.com. Thank you.

ZONDERVAN.com/
AUTHORTRACKER
follow your favorite authors